Ever Is
a Long Time

Ever Is a Long Time

A Journey Into
Mississippi's Dark Past

A Memoir

W. Ralph Eubanks

BASIC
BOOKS

A Member of the Perseus Books Group
New York

Paperback edition published in 2005. Hardcover edition published in 2003 by Basic Books.

All photos, unless otherwise noted, are the property of the author.

Photo editing by Vincent Virga.

Published by Basic Books,
A Member of the Perseus Books Group

Set in Electra by the Perseus Books Group

Cataloging-in-Publication data for this book is available from the Library of Congress.
ISBN 0-465-02105-0 (pbk.); ISBN 0-7382-0570-2 (cloth)

05 06 07 / 10 9 8 7 6 5 4 3 2 1

For Colleen, and the life we share.
And for Patrick, Aidan, and Delaney, who are the future.

Time is dead as long as it is being clicked off by little wheels; only when the clock stops does time come to life.

— William Faulkner,
The Sound and the Fury

Contents

Prologue

"Daddy, what's Mississippi like?"

My son Patrick, then six years old, once asked me that question during my nightly ritual of lying in his and his brother's beds just after turning out the lights. I wasn't sure what I should tell him about Mississippi, so I hesitated before I spoke; still I knew his question had to be answered. As I lay there with him in the dim stillness of his room, I began to weave a story about the farm I grew up on and the simple and sometimes idyllic life my family led. I don't remember exactly what I said to him that night. I do know that I shared with him one of the many happy memories of my childhood in rural Mississippi. When I finished my rambling reminiscence, his younger brother, Aidan, called out from the bottom bunk:

"Can we go there sometime?"

Of course I said that we could. "But we'll wait until you're both a little older," I told them, a statement they did not question, displaying trust as only children can. Patrick then smiled and hugged me; I kissed them both goodnight and walked out hoping that my story would bring pleasant dreams, yet knowing that what I had told them was incomplete. Like the trip to Mississippi, the full story would have to wait a few years.

Since that bedtime conversation, I have thought about what I should tell my children about Mississippi; I do want them to understand the world that shaped me, for better or for worse. I should tell them that the Mississippi I grew up in had two cultures: a white culture and a "colored" culture. Mine was the colored culture, one in which poverty was common and those who challenged the status quo and supported integration and equality suffered economic and physical reprisal, even death. I should tell them that the first cut in establishing your status was the color of your skin; if you were black, education had relatively little bearing on your place in society. As a letter to the editor in the Jackson *Clarion-Ledger* once stated, "If every Negro in Mississippi was a graduate of Harvard, and had been elected as class orator . . . he would not be as well fitted to exercise the right of suffrage as the Anglo-Saxon farm laborer. . . ." The conventional wisdom was apparent: Any white person was superior to any black person.

I should tell them about how my father had the title "Negro County Agent," was paid a fraction of the salary of his white counterpart, and worked in a tiny cinder-block building with a tin roof and no bathroom, in spite of being a college-educated professional. I should tell them about how my mother struggled to teach children from worn, out-of-date textbooks discarded from white schools. I should tell them that five years after their grandfather's death my family was given the back pay for the years he worked for the Agricultural Extension Service for less than a white man who had the same qualifications.

Still I know these details reveal only part of my Mississippi background. The integration and opening of Mississippi's closed society, sometimes called "Mississippi's second reconstruction" by historians, served as the backdrop of my life from birth until I left Mississippi as an adult. When I was born in 1957, the mindset among white Mississippians was that a baby born in Mississippi that year would never live long enough to see an integrated school. Almost twelve years later, I walked into an integrated classroom, but with a small group of protesters outside bearing brooms and mops, threatening to clean me out of the school like a piece of trash.

Through my parents' sleight of hand, as well as their professional status, my early childhood was left largely unscathed by the chaotic series of events that served as the setting of my childhood. If I wanted my children to have the complete story, I would have to tell them how my parents helped me escape all the terror of Mississippi in the 1960s.

But exactly how did they do this? This question had nagged at me for years, with my mother often just telling me when I posed this question, "It was hard, but we just did whatever we could." After pushing the issue harder, my mother would launch into several elliptical stories, some that reached logical conclusions and others that, at the time, seemed baffling and illogical. In spite of the lack of clarity, the conversations with my mother stuck with me. And with her blessing I began to search for the answers myself.

Just about the time my children began to ask questions about Mississippi, and I began to ask my own, came the 1998 opening of the files of its Civil Rights–era spy agency, the Mississippi

State Sovereignty Commission. In a strident effort to maintain segregation and white supremacy, the state of Mississippi established the Sovereignty Commission in 1956 to spy on its citizens and keep a handle on anyone, black or white, who challenged Jim Crow segregation. The commission recruited informers, harassed Civil Rights workers, and accumulated files about individuals that violated their privacy and could be used to destroy them, and perhaps even kill them. In short, the Sovereignty Commission was empowered to "do and perform any and all acts and things deemed necessary and proper to protect the sovereignty of the state of Mississippi, and her sister states, from encroachment thereon by the Federal Government." The actions and inner workings of the Sovereignty Commission were secret and known to only a select few in state government. Although it was a small agency, its influence on the culture, mindset, and politics of Mississippi in the late 1950s and early 1960s penetrated every county and town in the state.

During my childhood, I knew nothing about the Sovereignty Commission. From what I had now read about the commission and the newly opened files, I knew that this organization had worked to instill fear in Mississippians like my parents: well-educated, progressive-thinking African-Americans, more commonly known as "uppity niggers." Consequently, I began to wonder if the answers to the questions posed to my mother about Mississippi, as well as the ones I wanted to give my children, were in those files.

But I resisted.

Partly, I thought that the files would contain information only on activists who posed a threat to staunch segregationists,

not ordinary, middle-class folks like my parents who were
NAACP members back then, but could not be called front-line
activists by any stretch of the imagination. Subconsciously, I
was also afraid that what I might find would somehow tarnish
the stories I enjoyed telling my children about Mississippi and
defile my pleasant memories about growing up in Mississippi.

But one night I got up the nerve to check.

An Internet search took me to the website of the Mississippi
chapter of the American Civil Liberties Union, which I discovered maintained a list of the 87,000 names collected by the
Sovereignty Commission during its existence. The 124,000
pages of the Sovereignty Commission's work are only accessi-
ble in the Jackson, Mississippi Department of Archives and
History. Since I didn't have the desire to go to Mississippi, I decided this virtual exploration would have to do.

An alphabetical list appeared on my computer screen. I
clicked on the blue hotlinked letter "E," scrolled down the list,
and winced to find "Eubanks." Then I saw the names of my parents: Warren Eubanks and Lucille Eubanks, with my mother's
name misspelled as "Lucile."

I began to feel sick, as if someone had suddenly punched
me in the stomach. After walking away from the computer in
disgust, I sat right back down and stared in disbelief at the
names on the screen. Then it hit me: In addition to everything
else I had to tell my children, now I also had to explain to them
that the state of Mississippi had spied on their grandparents.

Since that night, I have been haunted by seeing my parents'
names on an Orwellian list of people who must be watched, lest
they threaten the Southern way of life cherished by so many

white Mississippians. After I tell my children about the spying and the harder-edged stories from my early life in Mississippi, the question that now stares me in the face is how much of Mississippi's past remains in the Mississippi of the present? My own mixed marriage, though no longer illegal as it was in the past, is still very much a taboo. In the early 1990s when my wife Colleen and I traveled together in Mississippi, we got our share of idle stares. But we also found ourselves on the receiving end of a few hateful acts, like an attempt to run us off a country road. We even got our own separate seating time for breakfast in our upscale bed and breakfast, an obvious effort to maintain traditional standards of Southern decorum. When the innkeeper found out that I was a native of Mississippi, her sour expression and pursed lips seemed to say, *"you should know better than this."*

When I do finally take my children to visit Mississippi, will they be welcomed there, or viewed as an affront to traditional standards of Southern society? Although I know that I cannot shield them from racism in American society, the Southern brand of racism is venomous and penetrating, particularly to an impressionable child. The Mississippi of my childhood was often nightmarish, riddled with scenes of intense poverty and despair, black churches set on fire by hateful whites, young bodies buried in earthen dams, and black men murdered by snipers while walking across their front yards. The all-pervading doctrine of the state was one of white supremacy rooted in the philosophical belief in slavery and perpetuated through segregation. The rules of segregation, in turn, were upheld with an iron fist purely to instill a sense of inferiority among the black citizens of Mississippi. And I was part of the group of people in whom a sense of inferiority was to be instilled, and at any cost.

Though the Mississippi I grew up in is different now from what it was when I was a boy, my experience is that there are still vestiges of those times lurking in unexpected places. For a child born today, the rules of Mississippi's segregated society are difficult to understand. I have already tried to explain to my children that once upon a time, in Mississippi and throughout the South, I could have been murdered for the crime of loving their mother. Although they accept that as fact, they don't understand why or how our marriage at one time could have been criminal.

Just as my sons don't understand the randomness of miscegenation laws, I sometimes don't understand why I feel so much affection for Mississippi. During most of my formative years, it was the closest thing to a police state as anything in this country.

Still, I want my children to know the joys I experienced growing up in Mississippi, for often I think that it has done as much for me as it did to me. Mississippi, the land and its history, inhabits and haunts me; its music and rhythms, both the joyful and the melancholy, have followed me my entire life, even when I tried to run away from them. I could never escape because being a Mississippian is the source of my inner strength. It lies at the core of my identity.

The memories of the Mississippi of my youth, though, are locked together with a sense of joy and wonder as well as fear and foreboding. Somehow I have to face up to these two Mississippi's: the one I love and the one I hate. It's time to stop running away from a place that is so much a part of me. Like my children, I, too, must know what Mississippi is really like.

PART ONE

Safe in a Sea of Calm

❖   ❖   ❖

Place opens a door in the mind.
—EUDORA WELTY

ONE

Mo'nt Ollie

The years have a way of providing what seems to be an infinite distance, yet somehow that distance helps me feel more intensely the joys of growing up in a small town in Mississippi. Time has made it possible for me to see what I both loved and disliked, as if both sides are placed on a stage in front of me to observe objectively. As I stand back and watch these two sides of my early life, I recognize that it was both the comfort and confinement of small-town Mississippi life that prompted me to choose a life away from it. The same forces that nurtured and made me feel secure also suffocated me until I found it unbearable.

There are times when I walk city streets and feel my little town of Mount Olive, Mississippi, tugging at me, telling me to come back. It's a good feeling, one that reminds me of people and places that I love: the calmness of fishing on the banks of a quiet lake, the smell of the food at a summer church revival, and a walk in the hills of my family's farm with my dog. There is no feeling of suffocation, only affection. But I have visited rarely since I left Mount Olive behind, largely resisting the pull and choosing to love the place at a distance.

"Place opens a door in the mind," Eudora Welty once said. As I tried to unravel the question of how my parents ended up on one of the lists of people to be watched by Mississippi's segregation watchdogs in the 1960s, one place helped open my mind to the questions of what made my parents and my family marked people: the sleepy Mississippi town of Mount Olive. On its surface, Mount Olive looks like an ordinary small Southern town: black and white, rich and poor, with a few people caught in between. "Mount Olive is a place where nothing ever happens," I remember writing to my cousin who lived in Mobile, Alabama, a place I thought to be far more exciting than my one-stoplight town. But as I began to bridge years of distance, I came to look at the world I knew growing up with a sharper perspective. Much more than I thought happened in that place where nothing ever happens. Tensions and excitement merely disguised themselves in a veneer of quietude, beginning with my own family.

Outwardly, we were an ordinary family: a mother, father, four children. Of the four children, there were three girls and me, the only boy, which felt like an unfair circumstance rather than an ordinary one to be born into. Like most of Mississippi in the 1960s, we lived on a farm, which was made up of eighty acres of rolling green pastures and dark rich fields planted in vegetables and fruit trees—all common in our part of Mississippi, except that we were black. My parents were college-educated professionals, and the middle-class aspirations my parents held could be viewed as both desirable and threatening to some whites. Like a number of black families in Mississippi, we farmed and grew cattle. However, we farmed not as our only means of making a living, but largely because my father was the county agent, or "Negro County Agent," as he was labeled then. My mother held one of the few professional jobs a black woman could have: She was a teacher at what was then a segregated school. Farming our own vegetables and raising our own beef helped my family make ends meet on the meager salaries dictated by Mississippi's system of segregation.

Mississippi's social and political system was set up to keep black people poor and uneducated. Even if you had an education, professional options were few, and my parents held jobs that were part of that limited realm. When I was growing up, it all seemed painfully normal, nothing exceptional; but looking back now, I realize how extraordinary it was. We lived a dignified life in an undignified system of racial segregation, largely ignoring the confines of that system. What I asked myself time and again when I discovered a tie between my parents and the Sovereignty Commission files was were my parents threatening because of the way they lived their lives? Along with the feared outside agitating advocates of integration, what I knew and remembered from overhearing snatches of adult conversations was that people like my parents had to be watched and kept in line, just to make sure they did not try to rise above their station and try to be equal to white folks. Together, my parents fit the profile of the dreaded "uppity negroes" who had to be kept in check.

My mother had bright auburn hair that complemented her creamy freckled skin. She drove fast, wore smart dresses with high heels, and had a mouth more flamboyant than her conservative manner of dress. Lucille Richardson Eubanks radiated a sharp, pointed warmth that announced "approach with caution." She held nothing back and maintained an undisguised disdain for Mississippi's system of segregation. "We don't drink colored water," she would tell us if we went to drink from the water fountain marked "colored." "Water is colorless, odorless, and tasteless," she would proclaim loudly as we drank the cold water from the fountain meant for white people, daring anyone to stop her. Surprisingly, no one ever did.

Someone had to balance out my mother's unrestrained boldness, and that job fell to my father. Warren Eubanks was a quiet, dark-skinned man, both the physical and emotional opposite of my mother. Though deceptively soft-spoken in demeanor and speech, he stood his ground with white people. Clearly, he approached the world of segregated Mississippi far more gingerly than my mother. In order to survive, he had to.

My sisters and I developed within these separate realms of the same family: the unrestrained openness of my mother and the measured, yet determined, approach of my father. Knowing that I would have to navigate the world as a black man, my father kept me rooted in his realm, taking me with him wherever he went, even to work. My sisters, Gretta, Sharon, and Sylvia modeled themselves more on my mother's brash personality and style, a characteristic that differentiates us to this day.

The tensions of those two worlds came to be balanced thanks to the farm. It threaded our lives together, for the land was both our passion and our pride and joy. Life there revolved not so much around our different personalities and mindsets, but more around the rhythm of the seasons and the work dictated by those seasons: planting, harvesting, pruning peach trees, moving cattle from pasture to pasture, stacking hay bales. Perhaps it was the rhythm of those seventeen years we lived on the farm that masked the extraordinariness I now see in my family, for there was a sameness in what we had to do from season to season and year to year. In the comfort of that routine, each of us developed our own unique set of inner resources to bring excitement to what was an isolated, staid, and ordinary existence.

I constructed an inner life for myself that shut out the daily chores on the farm. I wrote letters to children in faraway countries, read books about those places, and imagined myself there, even as I played games with my sisters. That same inner life also sequestered me from that topsy-turvy world of race and racism that controlled the Mississippi of my childhood. Shielded by the distance of years, I decided to go back to Mount Olive to take a closer look at a world I sometimes navigated with my eyes only half open. On a crisp fall day in 1999, I drove into Mount Olive, Mississippi, down Main Street for the first time in almost ten years.

If I was going to figure out what had landed my parents in the 1960s on one of the many lists maintained by Mississippi's Sovereignty Commission, I realized my search had to begin in Mount Olive. It wasn't exactly what I planned, for I thought I could figure out all the connections between my parents and the Sovereignty Commission through examining the commission's archives. There was much information in those archives, so much that I felt considerably overwhelmed. It was after spending hours in the Sovereignty Commission files, reading the grotesque tales included in its investigations, that I felt Mount Olive tugging at me. A voice seemed to say, *"I'll help you figure out all of this."*

I had always felt safe on the streets and roads in and around Mount Olive. And the people were friendly there. Now I knew this was the place that had shielded me from the hateful side of Mississippi, the very side I had been experiencing during hours of reading the Sovereignty Commission files. And I needed to feel safe again because I had discovered that some of that detestable, unsavory side of Mississippi lurked beneath these very streets during my childhood.

Up until the age of seventeen, Mount Olive was the only place I had ever called home. When I left to go to college, I never came back, and neither did my family. We sold our beloved farm when my father got a promotion that took our family to north Mississippi. As fate would have it, my childhood and my direct tie to my childhood ended at the same time. Two years later, my father was dead after a bout with cancer, shutting the door on my life in Mount Olive even tighter than before.

To my three sisters, Mount Olive seems like a vague memory, just an anonymous place where they grew up. I am the third of the four of us, the one who has returned to Mississippi the most. I was not able to shake free of it. All of us live in the East now, me in Washington, D.C., and my sisters in its suburbs and in Virginia. We all share fond memories of our farm and the town of Mount Olive, but for me, it's different. Mount Olive is forever imprinted on my senses and sensibilities. No matter how sophisticated I think I have become from my years in the East, there is still a bit of the wide-eyed country boy in me who grew up on a farm off a hot blacktop road outside of Mount Olive, Mississippi. I can't let that go. I guess that if I ever abandoned that bit of the country boy, I'd just be putting on airs and pretending to be a born sophisticate, which is something I am not.

When my parents decided to sell the farm, I went on a walk with my father to talk about it. I asked him not to sell; I told him that maybe one day I would come back, live in Mount Olive, and raise my own family on our farm. At the time I thought I would go to medical school, a career path chosen solely at my father's urging, which I naively thought would provide me the means and status to live the life of a gentleman farmer, a lifestyle totally at odds with being a black Mississippian. "Ralph, be a realist, not a sentimentalist," he told me. "It's a lot easier on your heart." We didn't talk about it anymore. A long silence fell between us. But what he said to me that day has stuck with me all these years. As I walked the streets of Mount Olive twenty-five years later, I finally began to understand what he meant.

The streets seemed practically deserted on the day I visited Mount Olive and bore the visible signs of graying decay that looms over many small towns throughout Mississippi and the South. Only a few of the stores I remember were still there, most overcome by the super Wal-Mart nine miles down the road in the town of Magee. Although Mount Olive appears to be fading from the lively little town it once was, no matter how much it changes, my vision of Main Street Mount Olive, Mississippi—my home town—will always shine as it did when I was a boy on that much-anticipated trip into town each Saturday.

There was a time when Main Street seemed to be bustling with activity, filled with wonder, people I knew, and exciting places to explore. My father and I would leave our farm on Saturday mornings in a steel-blue and white 1962 Chevy Bel Air to go to the feed mill or to poultry and livestock auctions on a vacant lot on Main Street, sometimes with my father serving as the auctioneer. Around ten o'clock the whistle of the Illinois Central Railroad would overwhelm the voice of the auctioneer as the train breezed through town filled with passengers from the North on their way South. When I got bored with the auction I would go to Powell's Drug Store and read comic books. Some I would buy, many others I would not, but I read them cover to cover nevertheless. Across the street from Powell's was the town's only phone booth, which I liked to play in since the light came on inside when you closed the door, a small treat for a small country boy. The phone booth was next door to the Green Tree Hotel, where on Sunday mornings, we drove to get our copy of the Jackson *Clarion-Ledger*, after a Trailways bus had dropped it off on its way to New Orleans.

Now the tree-lined boulevard called Main Street only looks weary and tired, like an old man breathing his last. The wrecking ball has long since torn down the Green Tree Hotel, which closed for good when I was in junior high school. Calhoun's Department Store, which I remember as having an almost Teutonic scheme of organization, with sharp rows filled with bolts of crisp new fabric and well-stocked grocery and hardware shelves, now has cheap, tacky merchandise from the store on the sidewalk outside. No one is browsing inside. Neither can I see any reason for anyone to want to go to the sidewalk sale either. The goods are out of date and out of season. It looks abandoned. Then it occurs to me that this store *is* abandoned and so is this town.

Mount Olive, or Mo'nt Ollie, as it is sometimes called in local dialect, sits southeast of Mississippi's much-romanticized Delta region and just a hundred miles north of the Gulf Coast, popularly called the "redneck riviera." Not known for rich soil planted in vast fields of cotton or casino gambling, Mount Olive was one of a string of tidy and proud little towns that U.S. Highway 49 ambled through during the 1960s before a four-laned version bypassed town and sent people speeding past rather than wandering through on their trips south to the Gulf Coast. There are no jook joints, unless you count "The Blue Goose," a little shotgun house outside of town that illegally sold liquor in this dry section of the Bible Belt. Around here, the standards of decorum have always been tight, and there is little tolerance for things that disrupt orderliness, liquor being at the top of the list.

The towns in this part of Mississippi don't have romantic names like the river towns of Natchez and Port Gibson or coastal towns like Biloxi and Pass Christian. The names are simple and humble, like the people who live in them: D'lo, Mendenhall, Magee, Collins, Seminary. Towns named Hot Coffee and Soso are thrown in to provide a small dose of local color, but a certain dignity seems to govern the choice of the names of other nearby towns.

Settled by whites in the 1840s, on land acquired by a treaty with the Choctaw Indians, Mount Olive anchors the northern part of Covington County with a wide Main Street that was once lined with 100 oak trees, many of which still remain. Until the railroad came through town in the mid-1890s, the area was little more than a scattering of houses and farms. A railroad surveyor determined the location of the town in the midst of this farmland by jamming a stick in the middle of a cornfield and proclaiming, so the legend goes, "This is where the depot will be." Just two square miles in size, the town was incorporated in 1900. By 1910, Mount Olive reached its peak population of 1,077; over the past ninety years, the population has dwindled only to 914 people. The entire town is only eight blocks long; ten if you stretch it.

The Piney Woods section of Mississippi, which Mount Olive sits smack dab in the middle of, lacks the starkness to inspire the blues or the river to give it an air of romance. The green, rolling hills of the region are filled with longleaf pine trees that were popular with loggers and were often used to build houses and barns in a style that is unique to the area. Cotton is grown here even today, but it never had the importance here that it had in the Delta.

Many of the first settlers of Mount Olive were Scotch-Irish: There were McNairs, Fairlys, and Buchanans, all white. Now those names are prevalent in the African-American community and, mysteriously, few white people carry those surnames. In fact, Mount Olive's most famous native, Tennessee Titan quarterback Steve McNair, is most certainly a descendant of those first settlers.

Mount Olive's Scotch-Irish roots run deep, for the eastern border of town is the unofficial boundary of a major Scotch-Irish settlement called Sullivan's Hollow. It has the notoriety of being dubbed by *Life* magazine "the meanest valley in America" because of the vindictiveness of its residents and its lack of tolerance of outsiders. Local lore states that when the men of Sullivan's Hollow talked about their relatives, they kept glancing over their shoulders, for fear of immediate reprisal.

Black or white, you never wanted to find yourself on the wrong side of Sullivan's Hollow. Especially if you were black. For a long time there were no blacks living in or near Sullivan's Hollow. This prompted whites to give the main town in Sullivan's Hollow, called Mize, the nickname "No Nigger." The racist reputation of the Hollow survives even now.

Even though the people of Mount Olive have last names, and possibly ancestry, in common, it keeps its black and white residents separated, like every other town in Mississippi. The dividing lines are distinct: Whites live on Main Street and the streets that feed into it, which are lined with period Victorian houses and porch-front bungalows; blacks live across the railroad tracks in "The Quarters," the home of the town cotton gin and a collection of ramshackle houses and shotgun shacks. The Okatoma, a creek whose name in Choctaw means "shining water," runs alongside The Quarters. Although the creek's name has a gentle meaning in Choctaw, in the spring after a heavy rain its waters are feared as it sometimes floods the homes and streets of The Quarters.

There are two other black sections of town: "The Jungle," which has Cotton Street as its dividing line from the white community, and "The Bottom." The Jungle was and remains a neighborhood of houses of various sizes and varying economic levels, a home to black professionals and factory workers alike. The Bottom is much more rural and is a series of winding roads, houses, and small farms set apart from town by Highway 35.

Set between The Bottom and The Jungle was the center of the black community: Lincoln School. Up until court-ordered integration in 1970, Mount Olive had two schools: one black, one white. The white Mount Olive Attendance Center was located "over town," as black people said; anything that wasn't in the black neighborhoods was "over town," meaning that it was the province of white people and off limits. Although the children from The Quarters were close enough to walk to Mount Olive Attendance Center, a bus picked them up each day, driving right past the white school to take them to Lincoln.

Lincoln School had two buildings: a white clapboard building that housed the first and second grades and a brick building that held grades three through eight. Both buildings had oiled wood floors that were perilously slick the day school opened and landed many of us in the office for the dangerous run-and-jump-and-slide stunts we did the first few days of school. In the third grade we got a brand-new gymnasium, a bribe from the white people to keep us from wanting to go to school "over town." By that time, which was 1965, Mississippi had instituted a "freedom of choice" plan for its schools, which supposedly permitted all parents, black or white, to send their children to the school of their choice, even the white school in town. Just as the white power structure wanted, very few blacks made that choice. What I heard most grown-ups say freedom of choice meant was the freedom to choose to have white people destroy you. There was a great deal of truth in that description, for those few who chose to go to Mount Olive Attendance Center eventually came back to Lincoln with broken spirits and tales of mistreatment by students and teachers alike.

After the eighth grade, if you went to high school, you were bussed to the county seat of Collins to Carver High, the only black high school in the county. Every day, buses picked up children of all ages on distant country roads and deposited them at Lincoln; another bus waited at Lincoln to take high schoolers another nine miles to Carver. Although school ended at three o'clock, children who took those same early morning buses had to wait until the bus arrived bringing the high-school students from Carver. As soon as the bus was spotted ambling down the road, children trolled the playground and the wooded area behind it for their classmates yelling "Collins bus, Collins bus," signaling that it was time to go home.

Now all that remains of Lincoln School is the gymnasium and the flagpole, which has the names of the class of 1950 inscribed at its base: Jeff Keys, Sarah McNair, Mildred Griffith,

Jackie Barron, Marcus Lockhart, Sadie Magee, Wardell Durr, John Edward Milloy, Annie Lee Benson, Tommie Snyder, Lee Roy Thompson, and Alex Barron. The day I visited, I read those names again and felt as if I was about seven years old, sitting at that same flagpole, running my fingers across those names in the concrete as I waited for my mother to finish her work in the classroom or to end a gossiping session with another teacher. But there was little else to stir memories of Lincoln. The two old school buildings burned several years ago and the landscape shows no sign of their having ever been there. The street that runs in front of what was the school has been renamed Lincoln School Road, but the tribute rings hollow. To me the street sign looks more like a tombstone, since as I walk around the place where I once went to school I feel like I'm walking through a graveyard.

Now the same gymnasium where I had Cub Scout meetings and made the winning basket in a third-grade basketball game is yet another factory dotting Mount Olive's landscape, one that makes men's and boys' pants. Rather than have white children attend a formerly all-black school, particularly one named for the great emancipator, Lincoln was closed when integration arrived. Although there was inadequate space for everyone at the school in Mount Olive after integration, the whites-only school board closed Lincoln anyway. After years of packing children into Mount Olive Attendance Center and into trailers, and pretending the school wasn't crowded, the town finally decided to build a new elementary school "over town." By then it was safe: Lincoln was sold and out of the picture.

Though the Mount Olive I once knew had withered and died, pieces of the town I once knew so intimately stood before me as I wandered around that day. Like the names at the foot of the flagpole, some were clearly recognizable. Others were hidden beneath the surface and were barely visible. But all the random bits spoke to me, sometimes loudly, sometimes only in whispers. And as I drove away from town that day, I knew the voice I heard was right. If I came back, Mount Olive would help me find my way through the Sovereignty Commission files.

At the core of the values of a small town like Mount Olive are conformity and submissiveness. Whites who came from farming families could never be accepted into Main Street society, the world of the Mount Olive Music Lovers' Club, or the private white community center, with its pool and tennis court. Blacks were relegated to their own schools, churches, and social organizations and had their own social pecking order. Blacks were free to shop and walk the streets of town without harassment, unlike in some Delta towns where they were severely restricted and could only come to town on a Saturday at certain times. Nevertheless, blacks were expected to follow whatever rules whites deemed were part of the social order, however randomly they were instituted. You used the side window at the Dairy Dip. You sat in the balcony in the Pix Theater in nearby Collins, even up until the early 1970s. Most important, you never walked through the white residential area unless you were the maid or the lawn boy.

At the center of the black social order were black professionals, like my parents: teachers, county agents, and small business
owners. Because I was the child of educated professionals,
some might say that I belonged to a privileged class of people,
blacks with a sense of noblesse oblige, if there could be such a
thing in Mississippi. My family was far from being part of
a privileged class: We were black, my parents' meager incomes
were barely above the poverty line, and we were outsiders. In
Mississippi in the 1950s and 1960s, as far as white people were
concerned, you couldn't get any lower than that.

Outsiders, Southern or Northern, were suspect, and viewed
as potential troublemakers who may have come to Mississippi
bringing ideas that might change a way of life that was comfortable to its white citizens. My family fit into the outsider cate-
gory, since my parents were not natives of Mount Olive or Mississippi, even though they were southern blacks. They were
both Alabama natives, born into a world much like Mississippi,
with its own set of racial codes. In addition to being outsiders,
they had been educated outside of the Magnolia state: They
were graduates of Tuskegee Institute, not one of the black colleges in Mississippi that bore the imprimatur of the state's
white power structure. All this marked us as a family to be
watched, both by local people and organizations such as the
state's Sovereignty Commission.

Although the black community embraced us, we did not live
in The Quarters, The Jungle, or The Bottom. We lived on our
own, outside of the social and racial conformity of Mount Olive.
And this was a conscious choice. Rural life in Mississippi in the

1950s and 1960s allowed struggling middle-class families like mine, college-educated people with low salaries dictated by racism, to live the American dream. Land was cheap. So, you could own a piece of land, grow your own food, and raise a family on your own terms, rather than those dictated exclusively by the prevailing social order. The independence of a rural life compensated black families, particularly educated ones, for what they lacked materially. Moreover, it served as a shield against the turmoil erupting all around Mississippi at the time.

Given my parents' personalities and intolerance for the strictures of segregated Mississippi, we were perfectly suited for the rural life. So, it was to a lush green farm of eighty acres that the Eubanks family of six retreated—a world of their own, an idyllic place where racism and intolerance had no place.

TWO

Car Wheels on a
Gravel Driveway

Outside my front door in Washington, D.C., is a tree exactly like the one that lived by the front door of our farmhouse in Mississippi. It is nothing exceptional: It's what my wife calls a "pfister," a broad-leafed tall and oblong evergreen shrub. In spite of its lack of grace, the tree captured my eye the day we bought our house, immediately taking me back in time to a faded photograph of my father and me standing proudly in front of the same type of tree, an image snatched from the family photo album the day my father died and hastily placed in a cheap dime-store frame, where it remains to this day.

Unlike the slim tree in my front yard, the tree of my childhood was broad, round, and green. In the photograph, my father and I are both dressed for summer; me in shorts and a polo shirt, my father in a plaid short-sleeved shirt and khaki pants. He had taken the day off from work to spend my birthday with me and given me a bright red bicycle. Although it was used, it shined like new. The poor man probably spent hours polishing it, feeling guilty that he was giving his only son a birthday present that was not new. But more than thirty years later, I can still remember the excitement of riding it down the gravel path beside our peach orchard. My father, the tree, the bicycle, and the house are now all gone; but I have the photograph and memories that run deep. Those memories took on a new meaning as I set out to explore how this world I knew so intimately fit in with one of which I knew little: the Mississippi that kept a network of spies to keep watch on its citizens.

I realized many years ago that actually returning to my family's home destroyed the sweetness of the recollections. Little things take me back there: the sight of a dogwood tree in spring, a sprig of red clover, the taste of freshly picked peaches. From something so small and tangible, I travel instantly back in time to a place that never leaves me.

This sense of place is handed down from generation to generation in the South. Childhood homes have meaning to most people, but for Southerners they have a special significance. We don't just call the place we once called home "where I grew up" or "my parents' house," Southerners often call it our "old home place" or "the home place," with an emphasis on the word *place*. Southern culture breeds an inexorable tie to a place or the land, since one is brought up with the sensibility that a specific place defines your very being. The home place is not just a place; it occupies almost a sacred realm, one that is unaltered by the passage of time and distance.

My father grew up in Choctaw County, Alabama, on a sprawling section of land that his family came to own through the Homestead Act. To own the 160-acre plot, my father's family had to build a house on the land, dig a well, plow ten acres, build fences, and live on the land. Five years after William Frederick Douglas Eubanks, my grandfather, fulfilled the requirements, the land belonged to him and his family.

The Eubankses held on to their home place for more than 20 years after my grandmother moved into town and no longer lived there. My family made annual treks to Alabama to pay the property taxes on the land. The place held such special significance in my father's family because after emancipation the Eubankses were the first generation of black farmers to own that land. My father's Grandma Julie once held court on the front porch of that house with her stories of her days as a slave, with all the children hanging on her every word. My father's sister, Glovina, and her children lived there for years to keep it in the family, but eventually they, like my grandmother, moved into town. The home place was left sadly abandoned but still in the proud possession of the family. Although I never thought it looked like much, I always knew my father's home place was beloved by the look on his face when we walked around it on visits. Even after the house and the farm had declined and became a financial albatross on the family, the sight of it never failed to give my father a boyish glint in his eye.

On Sunday visits to my grandmother's house, bracketed by a long car ride to and from Alabama, I can remember eavesdropping on conversations my father had with her about selling the home place. As he spoke, my grandmother would move her rocking chair with greater intensity as she gazed at him with her steely blue eyes. In the end, all my grandmother would say was "Brother" (everyone in my father's family called him "Brother," since he was the oldest son) "I ain't selling it." It took years of Sunday conversations like that one for my grandmother to relent and sell the farm. In the end, I never knew what finally convinced her other than my father's vigorous persistence.

My mother still makes what I call a pilgrimage to her home in Washington County, Alabama, in the town that was once called Prestwick. Her tie is so strong that although she lives in Virginia she maintains an Alabama driver's license emblazoned with the rural route address of her childhood home. My mother's family, the Richardsons, managed to keep their home place in the family, where it remains to this day. Though some have left, much of my mother's family live within shouting distance of each other and have either never left Prestwick or returned there after years of living away from Alabama. There are Richardson relatives all up and down the dirt road you drive down to get there, and the house sits at the very end of that road, something I always found unusual as a child. But as an adult, I came to understand why my grandfather built his house where he did.

Unlike my father's home, which had its legacy in slavery, a white man built my mother's birthplace. That man was her father, James Morgan Richardson, who dared to marry a black woman in Alabama in the 1910s. Jim Richardson built his house at the end of a road so that anyone who came there had no way out. If you came there to do him or his family harm, you faced his rule of justice, represented by a double-barreled shotgun. And my mother adheres to that philosophy, albeit slightly modified, to this very day.

As a young man, Jim Richardson liked to take risks and displayed an outward resistance to what was dictated as acceptable. True to himself, and in defiance of his family, he ran away to Mississippi to marry a light-skinned black woman named Edna Howell. No one knew them there. Subsequently, no one stopped them or questioned Edna's racial identity. Their vows were sealed with a wide, bright yellow gold ring, which my mother always wore on her right hand, that I always found beautiful by virtue of its simplicity. Yet its ordinariness masks a relationship that at the time was not simple at all.

What complicated my grandparents' relationship was that they chose to build a family as the forces of Jim Crow were in their ascendancy. At the time of their marriage in 1915, my grandparents' marriage was only discouraged by Alabama's state constitution. By 1928, the year before my mother was born, it was declared a felony. After my mother was born, the penalties for interracial marriage were set at two to seven years of hard labor.

In spite of the laws on the books, interracial relationships were common at the time; but intact mixed-race families like my mother's were rare. With the forces of law calling for the dissolution of mixed-race marriages, families like my mother's were usually torn apart. If the law did not intervene, social isolation and mob violence did. Needless to say, forging close family ties was no small feat, but somehow my grandparents made that happen. Jim and Edna had no master plan about how they would form a family. They just did it and carved out a place of their own at the end of a dirt road.

To build a life for his family, Jim Richardson cast his whiteness aside, moved to Prestwick, a thriving African-American community, supported the local African Methodist church, and lived among the black people who accepted him as one of their own. In the end, his funeral was held in that very church, though he was not much of a churchgoer. And it was only then that his family asked for him back: They wanted him buried in the Richardson family cemetery. "We had him all of those years, so we decided that if they wanted him now, they could have him back," my mother proclaimed with defiance.

Although my mother told us kids all about Jim (for that is what she always called her father) and his exploits in foiling the Klan and other angry white folks, I always thought he was black. Of course, he had to be in my mind, since my mother was black and all my relatives down that dirt road were black too. For the most part they were fair enough to pass for white; but my mother's family looked upon light-skinned blacks that passed for white with a disdain often reserved for criminals. Almost as bad were light-skinned blacks that maintained an air of superiority toward their darker-skinned brethren. If you were black, you were proud of it and didn't hide it. Having white blood didn't make you better than anyone else.

I understood this better when I was an adult and my mother began to open up. She told me that she, too, did not know that her father was a white man until she was almost six years old and heard someone call him "that white man." And it really did not all come together for my mother until she was seven and her mother died.

When my grandmother died, an offer was made by the town doctor to send the family away to the North to pass for white. According to my mother, Jim told the doctor that he wanted his children to face up to who and what they were, in spite of their designation as white children in the county birth records. So, the family stayed in Prestwick, my mother went to the black school there, and Jim sent her on to Tuskegee Institute, even though he knew he could never visit her there. "Are there other girls there who look like you?" Jim once asked her sheepishly as he inquired about her life at Tuskegee. She assured him that there were and that she felt perfectly comfortable at Tuskegee. Jim may have been a white man, but he didn't let his children grow up being ashamed to be black. Without deception, he understood the burden of race and color.

When I bought my first house, my mother gave me a painted photograph of Jim. It hangs near a black-and-white photograph of my other grandfather, the dark, proud-looking William Frederick Douglas Eubanks, as well as photographs of my wife's Irish and Swiss-German grandparents and great grandparents. But this prominence and openness with family pictures is something new. When I was a child, the portrait of my white grandfather was kept in the closet of my parent's bedroom. Though I did not know it as a child, I now know that the photograph's presence on the walls of our home could have led to questions about my mother's racial identity. My father must have feared those questions might lead to other questions, or guide people to the trail of my mother's birth records designating her as white. So, Jim's race was kept a secret.

Though my grandfather's race was a closely guarded secret, his influence had an impact on my parents' lives before and after they were married and even after his death. "The hardest thing I ever did was ask a white man to marry his daughter," I once overheard my father tell my mother. But I sometimes wondered if it was harder to live in the shadow of a man who so strongly shaped my mother's sensibilities. His image may have been tucked away in a closet, but his influence loomed in my parents' lives nonetheless.

Though they met at a church meeting and later at Tuskegee Institute in 1947, my parents did not get married until 1952. My father could not ask to marry my mother until he felt he could support her in the same way as Jim Richardson. And Jim would not have given his permission until he was sure that my father could do that. By the time my parents married, my father was working as a County Agent for the Extension Service in Lexington, Mississippi, a job he had moved up to from teaching World War II veterans after graduating from college. Jim must have thought my father had a future promising enough for his youngest daughter, whom he had brought up largely on his own from the age of seven. And he must have thought that he could protect her. Jim knew that when they moved to the Mississippi Delta life would be tough for them.

While my mother bridged the black and white worlds, my father only knew the world of being black. An outspoken black woman who both looked white and had no fear of whites would make her husband a moving target for white racists in the Mississippi Delta. Although my mother knew this, restraint, particularly holding back the sharp verbal retorts that often peppered her conversations, was something she had to learn; it was not innate. "Sometimes I have to save your mother from herself," my father once told me, referring to what he thought was my mother's sometime rash outspokenness. My parents came to live on our farm in Mount Olive after five years of living in the Mississippi Delta. Although my mother remembers their move as one tied to my father's job and their desire to be nearer to their families, I often wonder if my father was prescient enough to see the upheaval that was going to come to the Mississippi Delta. My mother was taught by her father to be outspoken, sometimes to the point of being antagonistic. Jim raised her in an environment where you held nothing back, white people were equals not your betters, and you voiced your opposition to mistreatment audibly and forcefully. And it pained her that in the Delta, she had to exercise restraint and keep from being herself just to survive. Their move to south Mississippi was one of my father's attempts to allow her to live in a place where she could be herself.

After renting a house in Collins, Mississippi, for about a year, my parents bought what my mother remembers as a ramshackle farmhouse. My father must have had a vision of what the house could be, and together he and my mother set out to make it a home that embraced their own separate concepts of place: my father's sensibilities from the first generation after slavery and my mother's from her family's legacy of white Southern land owners as well as her father's sensibilities about protecting your family.

When I rode on the backseat of our 1954 Ford Custom on a long trip, the hum of the tires on the blacktop would lull me to sleep, but I woke up quickly when I heard the sound of our gravel driveway, a sensation that I'll never forget. The hole in the floorboard of the backseat magnified the sound and eventually led us to get rid of that beloved car for our 1962 Bel Air. The soft crackle of the tires on the stones was the comforting sound of coming home. Whenever I hear rubber rolling on gravel, I can imagine being about four years old and pulling into the driveway of our farm back in Mississippi.

I told my parents when I was in my teens that I thought we should pave our driveway, since in my estimation a neatly paved driveway would have looked more elegant with our lush green lawn. My suggestion was not met with questions of cost and upkeep or aesthetics. The issue for both my parents was that you couldn't hear folks pulling into the driveway as they approached our house. This was especially important to my mother, since for her family they always had to hear as well as see who was coming. After an audible warning and checking to see who was approaching, the decision was made as to whether it was friend or foe. The next decision was whether you needed your shotgun or not. Although we never faced the incidents my mother encountered in her childhood, the basic principles of survival she grew up with had to be in operation for her to feel comfortable. For me the sound of gravel is comforting; for my mother, the sound is part of a survival instinct.

The house at the end of that gravel driveway never seemed small to me. I remember it as spacious, but when I look at photos of it now it seems tiny. When I close my eyes and try to picture it, I see the hardwood floors of our living room with the picture window, the piano on which my sisters practiced endlessly, sometimes in their sleep, and a wall of bookcases that held all my favorite books, in particular a six-volume set called *My Bookhouse* that included colorfully illustrated nursery rhymes as well as retellings of Greek myths. Just down the hall there was my parents' bedroom, with the closet that held my grandfather's picture as well as the smell of my mother's collection of leather high-heeled shoes. My sisters and I had rooms directly across the hall from each other, mine with a narrow but deep closet, theirs with a spacious walk-in closet where we sometimes played school on rainy days. What made this closet special was that we were allowed to write on its walls as much as we wanted. As we moved away from playing school, we documented numerous events on the closet walls, including the birth of my sister Sylvia in 1964 and the day we moved out of the house in 1973.

As in many families, our main gathering place was the kitchen, which had a 1950s-style green metal and Formica table, with checkerboard green and yellow tile to match the table and chairs. It was in this kitchen where we had all of our family meals, including my mother's seemingly endless supply of fried chicken, mashed potatoes, and warm chocolate cake on Sundays. The kitchen had a big window that looked out into the backyard, which is where my mother would have us play when we were small, so she could keep an eye on any mischievous behavior as she cooked dinner.

The door from the kitchen led to a laundry room, a coveted strategic station in the war games we sometimes played with children who visited. The game involved using the windows to launch water balloons or other projectiles on the unsuspecting party who thought an inside location in a game of war had no strategic value. The carport outside the laundry room was off limits in these games, so the door to the outside never had to be locked.

Beneath the front picture window there was a brick planter with neatly trimmed boxwoods, concrete steps, and a walkway, which bore our footprints at the end. The house was clapboard painted in off-white (bright white in the last years we lived there) with brick only to the window ledges. Almost an acre of lush, green, well-manicured lawn surrounded our home.

What the house lacked in interior space we made up for outside, since we spent most of our time playing in the nearby fields and orchards. Our peach orchard stood to the right of our house, and it was my father's pride and joy. In the spring it was filled with red clover and we had our Easter egg hunts there after church on Easter Sunday. The first peaches came in May and grew through the summer, until the end of July. The orchard was by far the favorite place for me and my sisters, Gretta, Sharon, and Sylvia, to play and frolic; it also served as the burial ground for our dead pets and animals. Whether it was a cat, dog, or even a dead hummingbird, it was given a proper Christian burial in that orchard, complete with sermon and mourners and maybe even a scripture reading from a red-covered Gideon Bible that one of us got at school.

The smells, like our chores, varied from season to season: In the spring, there was the smell of freshly tilled fields, peach blossoms, and, by mid-May, peaches. The piercing heat of summer brought early morning pickings of vegetables, particularly cucumbers; the smell of cucumbers on my fingers still summons visions of summer to this day, even in the dead of winter. On the way to the field to pick vegetables, the morning air was filled with the scent of honeysuckle mixed with the fragrant pink blooms of the two large mimosa trees that flanked both sides of the house. The fall brought the woody smell of pecans, which I collected in a sack or cracked in my hands to eat on the spot. And the sight and smell of hay for me brings back scenes of winter, since it was my job to feed the cows from November through early March.

When chores are done on an eighty-acre farm, the places for a child to roam seem limitless, and my sisters and I took full advantage of every bit of outdoor space we had. After the orchard, we might play in the stacks of hay bales in the barn, or wander down the hills through the cow pasture, where we kept about thirty head of cattle, to what we called "The Brook," which was actually a tributary of Okatoma creek. On a hot summer day we could wade, dam up the stream with rocks, or play with a water wheel my father built for us that we kept inside a hollowed-out stump. Down from The Brook was a little bridge we called Turtle Ridge Bridge, since we always found a turtle somewhere in the vicinity. The cows seemed to congregate at Turtle Ridge, so when we played there we often had to shoo them away, a task my sister Sharon and I loved since we liked watching them amble off. Near Turtle Ridge was one of the many places where in the summer we picked blackberries and wild huckleberries, often eating all that we picked.

A quarter of a mile to the east of our house was an old gravel pit where we searched for fossils, threw rocks in the pond, or just dug in the mucky red clay. My oldest sister, Gretta, would use the clay from the gravel pit to make sculptures and the occasional ashtray for my parents. To the west, on our property (the gravel pit seemed to belong to everyone and was even used as a dumping ground) was a long sloping red clay hill that we would slide down in grocery boxes. Since snow was rare in Mississippi, we imagined that sliding down a wet clay hill in a box was a lot like sledding.

Because my father was trained as an agronomist, we grew almost all of the vegetables we ate. My mother picked, canned, and froze vegetables all summer long, and we grew far more than we could ever eat. Rather than allowing the extra vegetables and peaches to go to waste, my parents made their friends and practically anyone who drove by welcome to anything in our fields or orchard. I remember complete strangers stopping their cars and commenting, "That sure is a fine stand of corn you got there." The reply was always "You can have as much as you want as long as you pick it."

My father's agricultural training was put to use all over our farm, and he was quite proud of the years of hard work he had put into every horticultural element of the landscape: our lush lawn, his rose garden, and the green rolling hills behind the house he planted with grass for grazing cows. Around the house we had all sorts of fruit and nut trees in addition to the peach orchard: fig, pear, pomegranate, banana. There were three pecan trees around the house, all of them grown by my father when he grafted sprouts from a pecan tree onto the native wild hickory nut trees.

However, the farm I remember as lush and well planted was not always that way. The house was just a bit more than a shell when my parents bought it, and the land was overgrown and not cleared for farming, not entirely unlike the land my grandfather homesteaded in Alabama. Until I looked at an old picture of my two older sisters and me on the steps of the house, I had even forgotten that the house remained wrapped in tar paper for almost two years. The loan officer at the local office of the Farmer's Home Administration refused to give my father the money to finish the house. He thought my parents should be satisfied just to have a house, any house that provided shelter for their family. If we had brick rather than tar paper, we would have been living better than the white farmer down the road, which in the 1960s was not acceptable in Mississippi.

As I remember the story, the loan officer's state supervisor went on a tour of all the farms in the county that had received loans from the Farmer's Home Administration. When he saw our house, and my father showed him all the work he had done, the state supervisor asked the loan officer why he wouldn't let my father have the money to finish the house.

Without a satisfactory answer, the supervisor said, "Give this man what he needs to finish this house."

My father not only finished the house; he beautified the land. Eventually, my father became an assistant county supervisor for the Farmer's Home Administration, and Mr. Whittington, the man who had denied him the loan, became his boss, friend, and quail-hunting companion. In keeping with the etiquette of black men of my father's generation, I never heard my father speak ill of Mr. Whittington. In the ten years they worked together, I doubt that either man ever mentioned what had once happened between them. Rather than use his energy to badmouth Mr. Whittington, my father put all of his effort into his work and creating a beautiful home for his family.

Our farm was much more than a beautiful piece of land, though. In many ways, it was a world unto us. Distant from The Quarters, The Jungle, and The Bottom. All families structure a world around themselves, designed to keep unwanted influences out. And the outside world was shut out from us when we were on the farm. We were exposed to it only when we read the newspaper, went to town on a Saturday, or went shopping in Jackson or Hattiesburg. Then we saw the segregated bathrooms, water fountains, waiting rooms, the neighborhood dividing lines that could not be crossed, and the racially prescribed codes of behavior. Perhaps because we were exposed to the brazen ugliness of segregation occasionally rather than every day, it seemed the exception. The life we led on the farm was what was normal. Just as my grandfather had built a house at the end of a road to survive a world hostile to his interracial marriage, we spent our time on our farm to guard us from unwanted influences that would tell us we were inferior because we were black.

We were removed, deliberately, but we were not completely isolated. My parents, particularly my father, valued personal relationships with people from all walks of life. From the county sheriff to an illiterate couple whose taxes my father prepared year after year, anyone was welcome at our farm as long as they followed my father's code of treating his family with dignity. It was through watching my father's interactions with people, both on the farm and off, that I learned how to build relationships. In those relationships, people became inexorably tied to place. In my mind, the people in and around Mount Olive remain that way to this day.

THREE

Mighty Fine People

*B*efore I journeyed back to Mississippi to delve into the Sovereignty Commission files, I spent hours perusing the list of names presented on the ACLU website, searching for people I knew: people whose farms I had visited, some who had visited my farm, or people I heard my parents discuss in daily conversation. Over several months, I compiled a list of names but found that they triggered only occasional sparks of recognition. Soon I realized that the names were tied to places as well. After being away for so many years, I had to return to the places I associated with these people for my search in the Sovereignty Commission files to have any real meaning.

On my first trips back to Mississippi, I spent time driving down country roads I had not traveled in years but felt as if I had left only yesterday. Rather than the gravel and dirt roads of my childhood, with the dust billowing behind the car and rocks flying under the wheels, all the roads are now neatly paved and marked with signs bearing the names local people gave them: Rock Hill, Mount Pleasant, Sunset, Ora Swamp, Hopewell,

Williamsburg, Prospect. Some have been named for their inhabitants or those who once inhabited them: Stubbs, Stroud,
Griffith, Easterling. The designated road names in rural Mississippi
seem a bit citified, yet the surroundings still have a down-home,
country feeling. Tall Mississippi pines, mingled with dogwood,
oak, and hickory trees, shade the roads, which roll and curve
erratically past fields of hay, corn, and soybeans and green pastures. The smell of pine needles drifts through the air, mixed
with the scent of freshly plowed fields. Both new and weathered
old farmhouses with dilapidated barns blend in with the scenery
and earthy smells, revealing a natural, unspoiled beauty and the
love all Mississippians, rich and poor, here have for the land.

Many of the same families I knew as a boy, or descendants
of those families, live in the houses that line these roads. Mailboxes bear recognizable names, some more so than others:
Ponder, Hollingsworth, Ainsworth, McNair, Magee. Perhaps
the Southern emphasis on social relationships is the reason
small Southern towns are described not only by their buildings
and landmarks, but also by the people who live, or once lived,
there. People are the very essence of life in small communities
throughout Mississippi.

My old home place is an example of how people and places
become intertwined. Although the Eubanks family has not
lived on that piece of land in over twenty-five years, people still
call it "the old Eubanks place," even though now little remains
from when we lived there. In tightly knit towns like Mount
Olive, you are never anonymous, even after you leave; your
mark is left there, just as the town leaves its mark on you.

The tie of people and place also plays a role in communication. If you drive down the streets and roads in and around Mount Olive with a native—whether you are on Main Street, The Quarters, The Jungle, or out on a country road—your traveling companion will be able to tell you who lives in just about every house you pass. During the conversation, with some gentle encouragement, you'll find out a little bit about the inhabitants of a household, along with a touch of local history and gossip. This happened to me when I went down the road to ask my former neighbor about the night a tornado destroyed my old house. I got an encapsulated history not only of that night, but also of the families who had lived in the house up until the time it was ripped from the ground.

As I listened carefully to the intonation of my former neighbor's voice, I detected a combination of reserve and openness; some things he would tell me about the people who had lived in my old house and others he would not. If his expressions moved in a slow, sing-song inflection, I knew if I wanted to know more, I was free to ask; but I would only be told if I asked. There is a message in a story told quickly and abruptly, that is missing several key details—"don't ask any more, 'cause I won't tell you." Such cadences and tones are the mark of a Southern upbringing. Nonverbal cues are part of Southern manners, because some things are spoken, and others are best never voiced at all lest they be thought of as rude.

Manners not only govern behavior in the Southern code of behavior, they bind a community together. In small-town Mississippi, manners do not consist of mere social niceties or

formalities; they are a moral code aimed at maintaining a defined social order. In a WPA research project on the history of
Mount Olive, Mrs. Ruby Huff Jordan noted that Mount
Olive's early settlers "brought to this location only the clean-
est type manners, in the very truest puritan type. In this small
town there is a 'Grooved way' to follow." That description,
written in 1936, characterizes Mount Olive as I remember it
in the 1960s. Manners set the pace of everyday life. Mount
Olive thought of its people as enlightened, more like Faulkner's noble Gavin Stevens and less like the conniving, poor
Snopeses of neighboring Sullivan's Hollow.

This grooved way influenced behaviors for people of all
races and stages of life. There was no separation of the public
and private selves: The image projected in public was a direct
reflection of whatever constituted a private life. Nowhere was
this more evident than in how children were to behave in public, for a breech of the town code of manners bore serious consequences. Let's say you ran down the street on your own rather
than with your family on a trip to town, spoke to an adult before he or she acknowledged your presence, or made a sassy remark to a teacher (one of the more serious offenses). For any
one of those infractions, you could expect a severe punishment. Your punishment was less for the actual offense, and
more for what it said about your family.

Though whippings were the most common form of punishment, your offenses might be punished verbally as well. A
whipping was over quickly, but a verbal punishment had enduring consequences. A verbal punishment was not abusive;

no, a verbal punishment meant that your parents shared the very substance and detail of your bad behavior with whomever they saw fit. As did the Ancient Mariner, your mother and father shared your tale of woe with anyone and everyone who would listen. That is, anyone and everyone they thought would keep you on the straight and narrow. Once I broke out in laughter in the middle of church during a prayer. Not only did I get taken outside for a firm reprimand from my father, but the superintendent of the Sunday school, Mr. Deen, also later came to talk to me. "Your Daddy told me what you did, son," he said in a tone that made it clear that he had the authority of a parent, since he knew my family so well. "You're not going to do that again. No, siree, we're going to make real sure of that." No parent wanted to have whispered behind their back, "those (your family name here) children just don't have any home training." "Home training" and the lack thereof was fodder for town gossip and brought suspicion and shame on your family. Families who did not train their children in the code of manners at home were uncouth, nothing but trash.

The code of manners extended to your outward appearance as well as your behavior. It was considered poor manners to wear farming clothes in Mount Olive Bank or to go shopping at Calhoun's Department Store; such attire was only suitable in the cotton gin, the pickle vat, or Polk and Duckworth's Feed Mill. If somehow you violated this standard of decorum, and circumstances required that you wear your overalls or coveralls somewhere inappropriate, the conversation opened with an apology about your appearance before you did or said anything else.

A Saturday trip to town required that one dressed up a bit, but not as much as on a Sunday to go to church, which had its own set of rules depending on your church. In our little country Methodist church, Mount Pleasant, hats and gloves were required for women and coats and ties for men. Even on the hottest summer days, and without the benefit of air conditioning, men did not remove their jackets or women their white cotton gloves. Once my parents were chided from the pulpit for allowing me to wear short pants to church in the middle of the summer, even though the shorts were part of a tasteful Little Lord Fauntleroy outfit that I remember being stiff and uncomfortable rather than an affront to any traditional sensibilities.

So, in Mount Olive, manners were firmly part of one's public image and maintained an order determined and defined by the people of the town. Manners sometimes also cloaked antipathy, racism, and violence. As the old saying goes, a Southerner is courteous and friendly until he is mad enough to kill. Mount Olive had a code of racial behaviors that was typical for the South, one of those being that black men and women were called by their first names, not by courtesy titles such as Mr. or Mrs. Courtesy titles were reserved for whites, many of whom never even addressed their closest friends in public without a formal title. The grooved way of Mount Olive, and the Jim Crow South in general, dictated that a formal title for black people placed them in a station that was equal to whites. This type of equality was unacceptable. Stepping out of that station generally was not allowed and might make some white man mad enough to kill a black man who insisted on being called "mister."

That said, my father was one of the few black men in Mount Olive called "mister" by white people. He demanded that respect from white people and he allowed only a few white men to be on a first-name basis with him. Even today, as I talk with people in Mount Olive and all around Covington County, people say to me, "I remember Mr. Eubanks," not "I remember Warren Eubanks." One white man I spoke with made the slip of referring to my father by his first name and then corrected himself. I was moved to see that the same respect my father demanded in life, he still had in death.

My father had his own code of manners, and at the core of his code was respect. He didn't ask for it; he demanded it. And, as a World War II veteran of the invasion of Okinawa, he felt he had earned it. His response to most racial indignities was, "Don't forget that I fought a war for this country." Like many men of his generation, World War II defined my father's very being. Even in a segregated Army he learned that a good soldier could earn the respect of his superiors and subsequently be treated honorably. He knew that with respect came dignity, and dignity could not be taken away. Nor could anything take the place of dignity. So it was with a soldier's ethos that in the Jim Crow South of the 1950s and 1960s Warren Eubanks went to battle to be treated equally. In his work as the Negro County Agent he could not demand equal pay to Arthur O'Brien, his white counterpart, an inequity that was widely known, since both men's salaries were published annually in the county newspaper, the Collins *News Commercial*. Still he demanded to be treated as the professional that he was and worked to have a stature in the community equal to, if not greater than, Arthur O'Brien's.

Insisting on equal treatment in Mississippi brought the same risks as demanding the right to vote; rarely was it tolerated. My father knew this from his upbringing in Alabama, as well as from the years he worked in the Mississippi Delta towns of Lexington, Mileston, and Tchula in Holmes County. Once he and a colleague had to move the body of a murdered black man, shot dead just because he acted like the equal of a white man, from the town square in Lexington. No one else would do it, but my father and his friend, Lowell Byrd, were brave enough to take the taunts of the white men who dared them to move the body. He and my mother even had to take up a collection among the community of black professionals there to help a family move north to avoid a band of angry whites. Had the family stayed in Holmes County, they would have been killed just because they asked a white man to respect their personal property.

Perhaps one black professional man demanding respect was not a threat to whites, since blacks only made up roughly thirty percent of the population of Covington County, and slightly less in the town of Mount Olive. Black professionals were an even smaller population, the largest professional class being teachers and the smallest being small business owners and people like my father and his three colleagues in the Extension Service. Or, perhaps whites wrote off his demand to be treated with the same respect as a white professional to his outsider status; a native Mississippian, broken in his youth to abide by the code of racial behavior, might not have made the same demands. Still, I believe that my father sized up the grooved way of Mount Olive, and Covington County, and worked its code to his advantage. From a young age, he made me an observer of how he did it. What he taught me was that any man, black or white, should carry himself with dignity; in exchange for behaving in a dignified manner, you would be treated honorably by those around you. In turn, you treated others honorably, even when they did not deserve it.

From the age of four up until right before I went to first grade, I went to work with my father. His office, which I viewed with great pride, was nothing but a cinderblock building, 14 feet by 18 feet, with a tin roof and a few windows to let the breeze run through on hot summer days. There was no bathroom; a wooded area nearby served that function. Above the front door to the office was an official looking weathered metal sign that bore the words "Agricultural Extension Service: Negro County Agent and Extension Home Economist."

As you walked through the dusty wooden door flanked by two windows, there was a concrete slab floor where desks and typewriters were packed as tightly as the limited space would allow. Three people, in addition to my father, worked in the office: Andrew Reeves, the Associate Negro County Agent for rural development; Mrs. Annie Barron, the Negro Extension Home Economist, the wife of Mr. Buford Barron, the principal of Lincoln School; and Miss Mable Newell, the Associate

Extension Home Economist. My father's desk was on the immediate left as you walked in the room. Across from his desk, in the center of the room, was a small typing desk and a dilapidated Remington typewriter, which was my spot when I came to the office. As my father did paperwork, I sat at my typewriter and did what I pretended to be my work, which were just silly stories that I made up or things I copied from a random magazine or newspaper that happened to be lying around the office.

If I wasn't at the typewriter, I sometimes sat on Miss Newell's lap. She was a large woman with a lap to match. One day I asked Miss Newell to marry me, and she accepted my proposal immediately. "Of course I'll marry you, Rallllph," I remember she told me. As only a Southerner can, Miss Newell stretched out my name as far as it would go.

When she asked why I wanted to marry her, I said that it was because I loved her so much. But more than anything I loved that soft, comfortable lap of hers and the broad toothy smile she gave when she stretched out my name. When Miss Newell did get married I was heartbroken and fearful of her tall, seemingly gruff husband, Lamar Thompson, who I later found was just as kind and gentle as she was. When Miss Newell left the Extension Service, I made do with the stories I made up on my typewriter.

Mrs. Annie Barron was the opposite of Miss Newell. Annie Barron was a slight, thin woman who seemed to exist exclusively on soda crackers and Coca-Cola. Her diet was at odds with her profession, for she was a nutritionist and home economist who advised women throughout the county on proper nutrition and food safety. The county agents encouraged subsistence farming, and the home economists showed people how to improve their diets through farming. This meant that her work, like Miss Newell's, centered on doing in-home demonstrations with women on canning, freezing, cooking, and nutrition in clubs she organized throughout the county. Miss Newell loved to cook and eat, and Mrs. Barron did not. But Mrs. Barron had a real gift for teaching others to cook. For that reason, she developed a strong network of "club ladies," as she called them, throughout the county with whom she regularly cooked, canned, and made jellies and preserves. Almost every day, she had a demonstration either with her club ladies or in one of the schools around the county, where she organized 4-H Clubs, so she was rarely in the office.

Mr. Andrew Reeves was one of my father's classmates from Tuskegee. He was a native of Mount Olive and our families were very close. Often both families had Sunday dinner at our house, particularly during his wife's recovery in a nearby tuberculosis sanatorium. Mr. Reeves was a constant presence in my life, since I saw him almost every day except for Saturdays. Mr. Reeves and my father had divided up the county, so they rotated farm visits between them, with Mr. Reeves working the northern part of the county near Mount Olive and my father working the southern part of the county near Collins.

The time we spent in my father's office was minimal, although it seemed that I sat at that typewriter forever. Mostly, we were out on the road doing field work, going from farm to farm, with my father putting his agronomy skills to work advising on crop rotation and diversification, recommending fertilizers for improved crop yield, and generally encouraging better land use. He also organized the Negro branch of the county's 4-H Club, gave advice on what to do with a sick cow or mule, and sometimes even treated the animal if he felt that he knew what medicine it needed. Other times he helped farmers vaccinate their herds against diseases such as blackleg, a fatal muscle disease in young cattle. I remember once there was a heifer with severe pink eye; my father cut out the cow's eye and sewed it shut. The farmer was forever grateful, since my father had saved his prize heifer and he told everyone he knew what a wondrous act he thought my father had done.

I made it a point to learn who lived around every corner of the winding country roads we traveled. The unpaved roads were dusty in the heat of the summer; after a hard rain, they were often muddy and rutted like a washboard. So, I learned where we were travelling not just by the landmark of a farm, but also by the feel of the car on the road. If we went to an unfamiliar part of the county, a part whose sights, sounds, and feels were unfamiliar to me, I would ask my father "Who lives there?" He'd respond, "that's the Alfred McNair place, and everyone around each of these corners on this road up to the fork is a McNair," or "that's the McLaurin place, and Mr. McLaurin has one of the biggest herds of Black Angus cows in Covington County." Sometimes he might tell me something about the crops the people grew or the type of cows they raised. I gathered all of this information together so that if I returned to that road or farm, its look and feel would be familiar and comforting. When I drive down those roads today, they feel just as familiar, even though they have changed, as have a few of the names on the mailboxes.

My father and I visited the farms of black and white families, even though his title was officially Negro County Agent. Like Mississippi's school system, its education program for farmers, the Cooperative Extension Service, operated on the principle of separate but equal. The work of a Negro County Agent included service only to black farmers and sponsorship of black 4-H Clubs. Since my behavior would be a direct reflection on my father and his position, a strict regimen rooted in the code of manners kept me in line and kept folks from saying "that Eubanks boy just ain't gettin' no home training." But most of all, my father thought there were things I could learn from being with him that I couldn't learn at home under the feminine influence of my mother and sisters.

What he really taught me was everything I needed to know later in life, particularly in high school and college, about navigating through an integrated world. At the time, I sometimes felt overwhelmed, for many of the lessons my father tried to teach went beyond what I could comprehend. Yet in spite of my inability to grasp my father's lessons then, they have all stayed with me somehow.

Before we left his office to visit a farm, he would coach me on how I should interact with people. "Speak up and speak clearly when you're spoken to," he often insisted, since he felt I was too soft-spoken and needed to be more forceful. He sometimes admonished me for not looking up when I was shaking hands or not giving a firm handshake. "A man judges you by your handshake," he would remind me when I was feeling shy. These social rules were as important as the more practical ones like staying out of the way of farm animals or not playing with strange dogs. And I interpreted and followed them as if they were designed for my personal safety, which in a sense they were.

The behavior he expected from me around white people was the same as it was around black people: perfect. There was no double standard. In fact, from my limited perspective I saw no discernable difference in the way you behaved around black people or white people. You showed the same face to the white man as you showed to the black man. No mask was to be worn in the presence of the white man. White people were not mysterious creatures to be feared or to be emulated; they were just people. As a result, I learned the importance of being yourself and not what people or society wanted you to be.

Perhaps because my father was only one generation removed from a poor farm family, it was especially important to behave as respectfully in a ramshackle house of a poor black farmer as in the home of a prosperous white landowner. Although he never said it outright, from what I observed as I sat quietly on the sidelines, I knew he believed strongly in upholding the dignity of people, regardless of status. More directly, he taught me that my status as his son, the child of black professionals, was never to be used to separate me from those who may appear to be less well off.

Whenever I could, for as long as I could stand it, I tried to act like an adult. It was hard, but I did it because he wanted me to, and I would do anything for his approval. As a result, I knew there were times when it was fine to act like a kid and other times when it was not. Rarely was I allowed to be the center of attention, nor did I expect it. On most farm calls, my father instructed me to sit quietly and just watch what he did. So, in what seemed like a cloak of invisibility, at least one that made my noisy, fidgety little kid side invisible, I paid close attention to his every move. Later, back in the car, I asked questions. We talked about the crops on the farm or what he thought caused a cow's illness . . . but most of the time we talked about the people and whether he liked them or not. "It's not my job to like people," he told me once, "but it is my job to help them."

When he had to go to a remote corner of some farm, the family would often take me into their home as their guest. I had to be on my best behavior then—the best, that is, from a four- or five-year-old boy. I remember eating sweet crumbly molasses tea cakes in the simple yet tidy kitchens of poor black families, homes that bore pictures on the wall of Franklin Roosevelt and Jesus Christ, and, after 1963, John F. Kennedy. I also sipped cold lemonade in the down-home elegance of the dining room of a white farmer, usually with the farmer's wife and occasionally with their children. In either setting, my hosts were to be treated with the utmost respect; no value judgments on my part were to be made about the social setting. Once during the ride home I made the mistake of mentioning that I noticed a hole in a wooden floor that I had to walk around to keep from falling in. "Don't ever judge people by what their house looks like," I remember my father said sharply. I don't remember very much else about that conversation that day, but I do remember the message: My father believed that any man who ridicules the poor is the one who is truly impoverished.

My father helped any farmer who sought his assistance. No one was given special status or priority and every farmer in Covington County knew it. In retrospect, he did much more than was expected in his job; Warren Eubanks could have earned his salary quite easily by working only within his defined territory, which did not include hands-on veterinary work or farming advice after hours. But doing things half-heartedly was not his way. Sometimes he even went out at night to help a farmer pull a calf, dragging me along to keep him company on the drive home to make sure he did not fall asleep.

When I went to school, the farm calls with my father ended abruptly. Although it was thrilling to go to first grade, school altered the rhythm of my life. Time with my father then centered around work on our farm rather than crossing the county together on our daily adventure. Though we still spent time together driving Mississippi from what seemed like top to bottom, like on our annual trip to the Delta to visit his old friends, those trips didn't feel completely carefree. As I grew older, other cares and concerns loomed as a backdrop to trips with my father. Little did I know that what felt like the jarring end of something in the mind of a preschooler only marked the beginning of bigger changes in my life and in Mississippi.

When I entered the first grade, Lincoln School, rather than the Negro County Agent's office, became the center of my social life. I was around adults less and around children more, which I welcomed, although I missed being the helpful assistant to my father that I had imagined myself to be. But there was a much bigger difference. My life, like every black child's in Mississippi, became completely segregated. The integrated, yet racially demarcated, social settings I was daily placed in with my father ceased. From August until May, every activity, with the exception of church on Sunday, revolved around the school. Because of segregation, there was little else; there was no Little League, swimming pool, or community center. The school was the community center.

The events of the school calendar—football, basketball, and baseball games, class plays, Halloween carnivals, Friday assembly programs, field day—gave a depth and texture to the seasonal regularity of farm life. Sports, plays, and assemblies were not just for schoolchildren and their parents; everyone in the community was welcome and often came, whether they had children in the school or not. Like many black schools of the time, Lincoln School reached out to make all members of the community feel that they had a stake in the success of the children at the school, which historically they had.

Lincoln School began in 1903 in a small building at the Saint Paul Baptist Church that cost about $300 to construct. Then, in the 1920s, the county bought three acres and a three-room school building, funded by Julius Rosenwald, a Chicago entrepreneur who directed the growth of Sears, Roebuck and Company. From 1917 to 1932 the building program of the Rosenwald Fund helped construct over 5,300 black school buildings across the South, 633 of them in Mississippi—more than for any Southern state with the exception of North and South Carolina. Rosenwald provided money and architectural assistance to improve school facilities for blacks across the South, largely in communities with inadequate schools. Since improving black education sometimes generated political tensions, Rosenwald also promoted white-black cooperation in the Jim Crow era, stimulating some support for black education.

To receive Rosenwald money, the local black community and the local white community both had to contribute funds. Although whites agreed to give local tax money to Lincoln School to match the Rosenwald grant, it wasn't nearly enough. So, like many Rosenwald Fund schools around the South, much of the matching local money was raised by a second tax by private subscription in the black community. The desire was so strong in the black community to educate its young that they chose to invest extra tax dollars in their children. As unfair as this may seem today, it speaks to the strong commitment this small community had to uplifting its young people through education. As a result of this financial tie, the school and the larger community surrounding Lincoln School became completely intertwined.

My first-grade classroom was in the original Rosenwald School building. It housed four classrooms: two sections of the first grade and two sections of the second grade. We sat at rows of long tables with worn green tops, telling of the minimal amount of money Mississippi spent on black education, even though it was separate but, in theory, equal. My time in the County Agent's office served me well in school, since I had learned how to sit perfectly still. Thanks to my diligent parents, I could also already read and write. For the rest of my fellow first graders, this was their first social experience outside the home. And for many of them, their first educational experience. There were no kindergartens or preschools.

The school principal, Buford Barron, came to dominate my school life, seemingly more so than even my classroom teachers. A large, white-haired man with a booming voice, he scared most of the schoolchildren into silence. In private, he was quiet, almost soft-spoken; but at school, he ruled with an iron fist. He called children from the playground by hanging his hand out his office window and ringing a hand-held school bell. There were two bells at recess: a warning bell and a second final bell. All children who had not cleared the playground by the final bell were swept away to the office—not by teachers, but by Mr. Barron himself.

During my time in the County Agent's office, I met lots of children, both black and white, as my father and I went from farm to farm. But when school began, I only saw or played with black children. I never questioned why the white children I played with on their farms and in their living rooms were not at my school. The bus that carried those same children drove by my house, so I knew they went to school somewhere, although I never saw where that was. Sometimes on our way home from school in the car with my mother and sisters, we would stop behind the bus as it dropped off my neighbor and playmate Joe Ponder, a white boy who lived down the road from us. We waved to each other, but the wave evolved into just a nod. A line had been drawn. I did not know why and, strangely enough, I never asked. It was clear that a social demarcation had taken place, albeit in a subtle way. Somehow it seemed rude, a breach of the code of manners, to question it. That was just the way it was. Period. But two events brought the dividing line between black and white more closely into focus: the murder of Medgar Evers and the assassination of John Kennedy.

Medgar Evers was an occasional guest at the home across the street from the school. This large green-shingled house, which belonged to Julius and Alice Magee, had a front porch that often served as a social networking point after school or after events at the school or nearby St. Paul's Baptist Church. Alice Magee was a marvelous cook, known far and wide for her cakes, pies, biscuits, and corn bread. If my sisters or I ever got sick at school, Alice Magee took care of us, a real treat because she always gave us something wonderful to eat, usually something freshly baked. An even bigger treat was to be her guest for Sunday dinner, an event that must have taken hours of preparation given the number of dishes she cooked and the sheer quantities of food prepared.

One of the occasional guests at the Magees' table was Medgar Evers. The Magees' daughter, Nan, was married to Medgar's brother Charles, and the Magees had made Medgar welcome to stop by to rest and to eat whenever he was on his travels from the far reaches of south Mississippi back to his home in Jackson. One Sunday afternoon, after a program at the school, a number of families went over to the Magees' front porch to talk. The children played a game of lining up and jumping off the front porch of the Magees' house. Medgar Evers was resting in a chair on the porch and got up and played our game with us, lifting each of us off the porch and throwing us gently on the ground. I remember his broad smile. I was quite taken with him, largely because he and my father had similar facial features and wore similar clothes: dark suits with dark skinny ties. After our game was over, I sat on his lap as he talked with my father. I have no memory of what they talked about, but I do remember just enjoying sitting on the lap of another grown-up man who dressed like my father and played with me in the same fun way.

I might have been five years old when this happened, far too young to understand why anyone would want to kill Medgar Evers. Now I know that playing with a group of children must have been a soothing diversion from his work at the center of the Civil Rights movement in Jackson. What came to be known as the Jackson Movement began with the organization of a boycott of downtown businesses. Later, the movement was taken to the streets through a May 28, 1963, sit-in at a Woolworth's lunch counter.

On the day of the sit-in, Evers alerted representatives of the media; as a result they caught on film the taunting of the demonstrators Pearlena Lewis, Memphis Norman, John Salter, Joan Trumpauer, and Anne Moody by agitated whites, the dousing of them with mustard and catsup, and later the beating and kicking of the demonstrators by the crowd. The scenes of peaceful protestors harassed by white thugs appeared on television screens across the country and began a mass movement among blacks in Jackson to fight segregation.

As Mississippi's field secretary for the NAACP, Evers had also been supportive in helping James Meredith become the first African-American admitted to the University of Mississippi. With tempers still running hot over Meredith's admission along with the publicity surrounding the Jackson Movement, among Mississippi's ardent segregationists Medgar Evers was a marked man.

Just two weeks after the Woolworth's sit-in, Medgar Evers was shot to death outside his home as his wife Myrlie and his children jumped up to meet him. Later, the weapon that killed him was found and identified as belonging to a man named Byron De La Beckwith who, it turned out, was a member of Mississippi's white Citizens' Council, the very organization that held white Jackson business and politics firmly in its grasp, making it impossible for the leaders of the Jackson Movement to negotiate with white business leaders.

The assassination of Medgar Evers led to a riot on the day of his funeral and a continuation of a boycott in Jackson, where we had sometimes shopped but now only rarely visited. Since Jackson was both out of sight and out of mind, the Jackson Movement was not part of my consciousness. What caught my attention was not local events but the March on Washington, which I watched with my parents on television. When I started first grade, my teacher, Geraldine Parker, had a bulletin board as you came into the classroom that showed Washington, D.C. That day she took us on an imaginary trip past the places the marchers had been so we could know what we had all watched on television. Right next to that bulletin board was a picture of John F. Kennedy, whom Mrs. Parker adored.

Right before Thanksgiving, Mrs. Parker's first grade did the weekly school assembly, your typical first-grade Thanksgiving play filled with songs about Indians and turkey dinners. Lunch and recess followed the assembly; but we were called in to our classrooms early by Mr. Barron's bell. Mrs. Parker came to the playground, with tears in her eyes, to line us up.

Back in the classroom, Mrs. Parker asked us all to be quiet and to put our heads on our desks. She then told us that President Kennedy had been shot. Mrs. Parker began to sob, and I remember her saying, "They killed him because he wants Negroes to be free." I wasn't sure what this meant, but I knew it had something to do with Washington, D.C., and the march she had told us about.

School was dismissed, and I went with my mother across the street to Alice and Julius Magee's house, where there was a television. In solemn quiet, I gathered on the porch with my sisters and some other teachers' children. No one played or talked; we sat. Suddenly the quiet was disrupted by shouts and cheers coming from an adjacent road. We jumped off the porch and saw that the noise came from a school bus filled with white children. It happened to be the very same school bus that brought my neighbor, Joe Ponder, to and from school.

They yelled that day: "They got him! Yay! They finally got him!"

The cheers of the white children on the school bus blended in with the chaotic and jumbled reports we heard from the television in the Magee living room and Mrs. Parker's sobs, which we could hear on the porch. Why were these children cheering? How could they cheer? I couldn't understand that when I looked at how this event had shaken all the people around me. It didn't make sense.

I learned from my parents that the cheering white children on that school bus were glad that Kennedy was dead because the Kennedy administration pushed for the integration of the University of Mississippi, or "Ole Miss." A year later, James Meredith's presence at Ole Miss still evoked Kennedy hatred in Mississippi, and this hatred inspired the governor's race at that time. Just weeks before the Kennedy assassination, the Mississippi governor's campaign was filled with virulent anti-Kennedy rhetoric. Paul B. Johnson won the election, and I thought he had won it based on his campaign song, which seemed to be in heavy rotation on every radio station in the state. Much to the irritation of my parents, my sisters and I even used to sing the chorus together when it came on the radio:

Stand up for Johnson, sing out for Paul!
Stand up for Johnson, best man of all!

But we had no idea what the second verse of the song meant:

He's strong for segregation and on that we'll all agree
In spite of Little Brother [Robert Kennedy], he will keep
    our sovereignty
He proved his faith and courage and was master of his fate
When they tried to make the campus but he stopped
    'em at the gate.

Johnson ran as "Tall Paul" because he had "stood tall" in the schoolhouse door when Kennedy forced the integration of Ole Miss. Like the verse in his campaign song, many of Johnson's political ads on radio and in the newspaper, as well as editorial page endorsements of Johnson, made use of a hate-Kennedy message that was effective enough to get him elected. One campaign poster showed Ole Miss's Colonel Rebel kicking John Kennedy and carried the caption "Forget, Hell! I'm Standing with Paul Johnson." Not to be outdone, Mississippi's Republican Party had large posters all over the state that proclaimed "KOK: Knock Out Kennedy."

My sisters and I had memorized the chorus of Johnson's campaign song, but the jubilant white children on that bus on November 22, 1963, had been filled with the poison that Johnson and others had been spewing all around Mississippi for weeks. Often I think it was those cheering children who made me read more so that I could understand some of the events that were taking place around me, even though much of what I read frightened me. The coverage of the Kennedy assassination certainly led me to read more of the newspaper than just the comics. Soon the pages of the Jackson *Clarion Ledger* began to bring news of outside agitators who were coming to Mississippi for the summer of 1964. One headline read that "integration forces" were leading the United States toward socialist goals.

The idea of socialists coming to Mississippi was confusing, because as far as I knew socialists and communists existed in Russia behind the Iron Curtain I had heard about in television commercials for Radio Free Europe. That was a long way from

Mississippi. According to what I read in *Life, Jet,* and *Ebony,* these people who were coming to Mississippi were from the North, not Russia. Maybe they talked fast and had that funny accent, like my friend Van Weathersby's cousins from New York, but they weren't the menace I knew the Russians were, like Khrushchev, who I had heard wanted to destroy the United States. But I did understand that these Northerners wanted to stop things from happening in Mississippi, like the murder of Medgar Evers. That had to be a good thing, but I had no idea what lay ahead for those outsiders. And, as far as I could understand it, all of this happened outside the world of Mount Olive, Lincoln School, and my little farm. The images of the marches and mass meetings felt as distant as dispatches from a war in a foreign country. I was seven years old and Freedom Summer had little to do with how we lived or what my parents did every day. As I grew up, and began to look back at those years, I would understand how wrong I was.

FOUR

Magnolias and Mayhem

M emory must be informed by history, lest history can become distorted when viewed purely through the lens of memory. As I look back on the Mount Olive of my childhood, the people, and my family's ties and relationships there, I have come to realize that another Mississippi existed outside of my family's rambling eighty acres, one that my memory distorts because it was shuttered out by design. As a child, I caught glimpses of that other Mississippi, the one that is now part of the history of the 1960s, and saw just enough of it to turn away in fear. I retreated into the safer world that was created for me. More than I ever knew, the Mississippi of my memory wraps itself around the historical Mississippi.

Mississippi has always been a place with its own mindset, one that looked with suspicion on outside influences. From the antebellum era through the early 1960s, Mississippi stood as a world unto itself, what historian James Silver called "the closed society," and others called "the Magnolia curtain." In trying to come to grips with the mindset of white Mississippians, Silver's friend, fellow historian, and native Mississippian David Donald wrote to him:

> The Mississippian has always lived in a self-contained world. . . . When he traded it was with other Mississippians. When he read, it was his own local newspapers, edited by Mississippians. When he got an education, it was at Mississippi colleges where Misssippians taught. . . . These people have no idea of a world beyond themselves.

James Silver, a historian on the faculty of the University of Mississippi, in the years following this letter, wrote a book entitled *Mississippi: The Closed Society*. To read Silver's book today is to step back in time to the era my parents knew, for he chronicles the people and cultural antecedents that made Mississippi a place that once existed as a unique culture unto itself, one that wanted no part of broader American culture. Mississippi's political establishment took advantage of this provincialism and scared white citizens away from influences outside the state's borders, particularly where racial progress was concerned. The Delta, the part of Mississippi my parents left behind to come to our farm, adhered to the closed society mindset to an exaggerated extreme. Had my parents remained in the Delta, the Mississippi of my childhood memory would, without a doubt, have been radically different.

From what James Silver wrote, as well as what I remember from my father's stories, Mississippi Delta whites displayed little tolerance for black men who aspired to be landowners or professionals. Consequently, the self-contained life my family led in Mount Olive, apart yet part of the wider closed society, was almost impossible to attain in the Mississippi Delta. The Delta thrived on a blend of random customs and violence, which grew during the post–World War II years when my father, and later my mother, lived there and imploded in the years after they left.

When my father graduated from Tuskegee in 1948, the only professional job he could find was teaching high school classes to World War II veterans in the Delta. At the time, the belief among blacks in the South was that it was against the law for a black man to pass a white man on the highway in Mississippi. My father's friends at Tuskegee believed that this law was enforced unmercifully in the Delta, despite the fact that no such law ever existed on the books. Still, this piece of folklore demonstrates how violence against blacks became a way of life in the Delta and across Mississippi, so much so that people thought specific types of ill treatment were defined by law. Yes, random and illogical Jim Crow laws existed in Mississippi. The practice of discrimination anticipated and exceeded the laws, and as a result there was relatively little distinction between what was law and what was local custom. Life behind what was sometimes called "the magnolia curtain" rarely made sense, with both laws and customs enforced with equal vigor.

By 1955, when my parents were married with two children, white intimidation of blacks mounted in the wake of the *Brown* versus *Board of Education* decision by the

Supreme Court outlawing segregated schools. Buoyed by the *Brown* decision, blacks mounted voter registration campaigns in communities across the state in late 1954 and 1955. Whites responded by attempting to frighten blacks into submission with miscellaneous acts of violence and intimidation, such as jailing a black man for passing a white man on the highway or shooting a black service-station attendant over the amount of gas he pumped. Around this same time, a white man in the Delta remarked to journalist David Halberstam in an interview, "There's open season on the Negroes now. They've got no protection, and any peckerwood who wants can go out and shoot himself one." This steady stream of haphazard white-on-black violence must have made my parents begin to question whether the Delta was the right place for them to raise a family.

The most infamous incident of violence that summer was the murder of fourteen-year-old Emmett Till, in Tallahatchie County, up the road about sixty miles northwest of where my parents lived in Holmes County. Emmett Till was visiting the town of Money, Mississippi, from Chicago and was unaccustomed to the severe segregation he encountered in Mississippi. When he showed some local boys a picture of a white girl who was one of his friends back home and bragged that she was his girlfriend, one of them said, "Hey, there's a white girl in that store there. I bet you won't go in there and talk to her." Emmett went in and bought some candy. As he left, he said, "Bye baby" to the wife of the storeowner and allegedly wolf-whistled at her. A few days later two men abducted Emmett from his uncle's home and murdered him, then tied his body to a cotton-gin fan and threw it in the Tallahatchie River. The men who murdered Emmett Till were never convicted.

Closer to home, that same summer, friends of my parents admonished a white neighbor for driving on their yard, since he was leaving tire ruts in the grass. Shots rang out and the white neighbor wounded the wife of my parents' friend. The threats continued until the couple had to leave town, leading the black community of Lexington, Mississippi, to raise enough money to send them to Chicago. My parents gave the couple $100, a considerable sum in 1955, and agreed to take care of their house until it could be sold. After my parents and my two sisters moved into the house, the white neighbor continued to drive across the yard, signaling to my parents that the time had come for them to leave as well, which they did.

While life in the Delta was behind them, my family still lived in the midst of a tightly controlled world. South Mississippi may have lacked the strong provincialism of the Delta, but it was still Mississippi. What made it different was that whites were less threatened in South Misssissippi, where blacks were in the minority, unlike in the Delta, which was majority black.

As integration began outside of the South in the wake of the *Brown* decision, white Mississipians became even more ardently determined to maintain their self-controlled, racially segregated world. Across Mississippi, books were banned from schools, particularly any book that expressed discontent with segregation. Television programs were also cut off when people or ideas appeared that were counter to the prevailing social norms. Up through the mid-1960s, the broadcast message "Sorry, cable trouble" appeared on television screens across Mississippi with some regularity, used to keep people as diverse as Thurgood Marshall and Nat King Cole (shown singing with Peggy Lee) off Mississippi television screens.

Censorship was not limited to television. The most powerful newspapers in the state, the Jackson *Clarion-Ledger* and its sister evening paper the *Jackson Daily News*, spun national news as they felt Mississippi should see it and told Mississippians what they should think. Owned by the powerful Hederman family, before and during the Civil Rights era, the *Clarion-Ledger* and *Jackson Daily News* not only censored news, they also helped perpetuate segregation and inflame segregationists by the way they reported the news. Reporters were largely forbidden from covering the Civil Rights movement. Editorials in both Hederman papers railed against integration, with warnings against "the mongrelization of the human race" in specific pieces on the topic. Representative of the content of the Hederman newspapers is this front-page headline, which appeared after the 1963 March on Washington: "Washington is Clean Again With Negro Trash Removed."

The racist tone of the Hederman papers, as well as Mississippi's fierce provincialism, made the Magnolia State a breeding ground for extremist groups devoted to maintaining segregation. In time, a new organization took hold of the hearts and minds of white Mississippi: the Citizens' Council. Established as one of the first arms of organized resistance to integration in the wake of the *Brown* decision, the ideology of the Citizens'

Council was grounded firmly in white supremacy. Unlike the Ku Klux Klan, the Citizens' Council did not advocate violence as a means of fighting integration, though it certainly helped encourage it by the literature it disseminated to its members and into the public schools. A crudely printed booklet entitled "Black Monday" by Tom P. Brady became the handbook for the Citizens' Council Movement. Its guidelines for saving Mississippi from the *Brown* decision included the popular election of Supreme Court justices, a program for youth on the "facts of ethnology," the creation of a state exclusively for blacks, and, if necessary, the abolition of public schools.

With the support of the Hederman-owned newspapers, the Citizens' Council became the watchdog of the state's public schools, colleges, and universities, as well as a powerful force in Mississippi politics. Before long, the Citizens' Council had Mississippi's political establishment firmly in its grasp. Then it made an astute political move.

Through the intense lobbying, combined with general hysteria among white legislators about integration, the Citizens' Council pushed for the creation of the Mississippi State Sovereignty Commission. Although it began as a tool to "tell the truth" about Mississippi and its way of life to the rest of the world, the main impact of the Sovereignty Commission was to put a chokehold on anything and everything related to integration. Quickly, the Sovereignty Commission moved from public relations to spying on citizens, trying to uproot anyone or anything that threatened to open up Misssissippi's closed society to integration. And the Citizens' Council received a source of state funding from the Sovereignty Commission for developing more propaganda for their cause.

For my entire childhood, the Sovereignty Commission was a powerful force in Mississippi, though I remained blissfully ignorant of its existence. One whole paragraph was devoted to the Sovereignty Commission in my middle-school Mississippi history book, but I only discovered its existence when I picked up the very same book as an adult. Most Mississippians knew little of the Sovereignty Commission, since its meetings and activities, though publicly funded, were secret.

In spite of attempts to cut off certain television shows, the censoring of information in the *Clarion-Ledger*, and the forces of the Citizens' Council and the Sovereignty Commission, I knew that change was in the air across Mississippi. A child in 1964, even one as young as seven, as I was, could feel the tremors that were bringing those changes. All around Mount Olive, we were surrounded by hotspots of the Civil Rights movement in Mississippi: Jackson and Canton to the north of us, which were centers of NAACP and SNCC activities, and Hattiesburg and McComb to the south, both of which were embroiled with bitter boycotts and voter registration battles. In Hattiesburg, Vernon Dahmer gave his life in a 1966 firebombing so that black people in the surrounding counties could register to vote. In McComb and Canton, and all around Mississippi, Bob Moses and other activists from SNCC pushed local people into action for voting rights and equality. As I look back through the lens of history, what happened right around me transformed Mississippi. Yet, all I could know, and all my parents wanted me to know, was the world directly within my view. It was a censorship designed to protect rather than to disguise the truth. Still, part of my world-view included people who were involved with the Civil Rights movement, though I didn't completely realize it.

Like most isolated rural people, I learned about the events of the Civil Rights movement from newspapers, magazines, and television. I had read everything I could about the Free-dom Rides, the marches, the demonstrations, and the murders. I knew what had happened to Medgar Evers, although my fam-ily never talked about it. But when I overheard my father telling my mother that he had to go to Neshoba County for work, I remember becoming really scared. I had read in *Life* magazine about the three Civil Rights workers murdered there. If my father went, would they burn his car and bury him, like those three young men I saw pictured in *Life*?

And when my father and I drove through Selma, Alabama, late one night in October 1965 on our way to a homecoming football weekend at Tuskegee, I replayed in my mind the televi-sion pictures of what happened on the Edmund Pettus Bridge just months before. Would that happen to us, I thought? The im-ages from the news were so vivid and sometimes scared the life out of me when I thought of them at night, whether alone on the backseat of a car or in my room when I heard the occasional car turn around in our driveway.

In time, what I learned to do was shut out the images from the news that scared me. I'd race over pages in magazines or leave the room during certain parts of the evening news. As I grew older, into my teens, the racially charged atmosphere

I artfully avoided stared me in the face. Now, as a grown man, I had read enough of the Sovereignty Commission files to know there was a truth I could no longer deny. Both my personal history and the history of Mississippi had to be at work in my mind to understand it.

I could no longer just skip the page.

PART TWO

Terror and Magnificence

❖   ❖   ❖

If there is anything that makes Southerners distinctive from the main body of Americans, it is a certain burden of memory and a burden of history. . . . I think sensitive Southerners have this in their bones, this profound awareness of the past.

— WILLIE MORRIS

FIVE

"The Names Included
in This File . . ."

*I*n silence I poised myself in front of a computer screen to begin my search for the pages I skipped over as a child. Though the images remain nestled in my mind, I now had to put the words with the pictures. As the words appeared on the screen, magically the pictures came back. Except now they were no longer interrupted by my hurriedly rustling past them.

Although virtually sheltered from this rougher, hostile side of Mississippi I now faced, it always loomed quietly, and sometimes not so quietly, in the background of my childhood. Though my youthful naiveté made the climate of antagonism difficult to grasp, I counted on being protected from it. I devoured the news of the Civil Rights struggle unraveling in Mississippi, yet shut out many of the gruesome details. As long as my mind kept the closet door shut, the monsters lurking in the towns all around me would lay quietly chained in the corner where they couldn't reach the door to force it open.

During my years of living outside of Mississippi as an adult, I continued to keep the monsters in the closet. I even thought I had made peace with the Mississippi that frightened me, accepting it as one might an eccentric relative that you can't change but love just the same because there is something there to love. And my love of Mississippi steadied itself on my love of its land and landscape, creating a myth based on a personal Southern sense of place yet still rooted in the romanticized Southern mindset I often derided. In the end, I realized that I had only avoided facing the truth.

As a Southern expatriate, time mellowed my memories of Mississippi and its madness. The passage of each year I lived apart from my home state smoothed out the rough edges. As the years collided, I came to view my personal history through a gauzy lens that memory both sharpened and distorted, caught somewhere between memory and forgetting. Only occasionally when meditating on my Mississippi past did memories fall into my field of vision with clarity without being blurred by my own personal myth of the South. It was my children's pointed questions about my childhood that made me think more objectively about the past, that summoned up memories of the hostile, suspicious, and violent Mississippi I continually pushed out of my mind's eye, both as a child and as an adult. The cold, hard truth that the state of Mississippi spied on my parents propelled the past into a different light, sharper, less romanticized, and more realistic.

In spite of a consciousness of the Civil Rights movement, I had made the choice to smother the lingering personal questions I had about those turbulent times. How did my parents navigate their way through Jim Crow Mississippi, particularly my father, a dark-skinned black man who was married to the whitest-looking black woman you ever did see, a woman who had to change the racial designation on her birth certificate from "white" to "colored"? What inspired them to face the indignities of segregation, yet maintain their dignity? Most of all, how had they managed to enable my sisters and me to escape relatively unscathed from much of the turbulence of those times? It was almost as if they had constructed a fortress around the four of us; but I dared not ask how they built it, lest I appear ungrateful for the gift of a normal, relatively undisturbed childhood.

Time also led me to take a look at my parents' involvement in the Civil Rights movement. During the 1950s and 1960s, black professionals, particularly educators, were reluctant to get involved with the movement. Medgar Evers once lamented, "as much good as the NAACP has done to make opportunities greater for teachers who once made $20 a month and are making up to $5,000 a year now, we don't get their cooperation."

Unlike many middle-class blacks, my parents were supporters of the Civil Rights movement. They were not activists on the front lines, however. They were proud card-carrying NAACP members and supported the movement actively, yet quietly. The white power structure dared them to vote and raise their family decently; they chose to defy it by doing both. In Mississippi at the time, that alone was a subversive act. In no way could either of my parents be called cowardly; they were not demonstrators or marchers. Those forms of activism were left to others.

On the first national celebration of Martin Luther King's birthday, I even raised the issue of my parents' level of involvement in the Civil Rights movement in a conversation with my sister, Sharon. As we drove across Washington's Fourteenth Street Bridge that day, we discussed the significance of the holiday to the children of the middle class, people like us who benefited the most by the work of King and those who marched with him on the front lines. When I asked Sharon how she thought our parents were involved, she quickly cut me off, "We were children then, and Mom and Daddy made the right choice in putting us first, not doing something that could get them and us killed." I really couldn't argue with that; our lives certainly would have been more fractured and chaotic had my parents been movement people. Without a stable, safe home life as a foundation, who knows where my fortunes would have turned? Still I wanted to know more about those years and what my parents did to cope with the challenges of the times. It was particularly important now that I was a parent myself. But after that conversation I felt alone in my search for knowledge of the past, my history. I didn't want to drown in it, but I did want to know how to use it to help me in the way I lived now.

When I began to explore the Sovereignty Commission files, what I found started to fill in the gaps in this history. In spite of the security of our little farm, the world my sisters and I felt safe in wasn't so safe after all. Middle class or dirt poor, activist or Uncle Tom, the eyes of the Sovereignty Commission were upon you. Warren and Lucille Eubanks weren't marching the streets of Jackson or in small Delta towns, but even their smallest activities were deemed worthy of being watched by the state. Had they been more openly active in the movement, the sovereign state of Mississippi would have ratcheted up their surveillance. They would have moved from being on the Commission's seemingly innocuous list of suspicious people to the list that was turned over to a local sheriff who would then decide his own course of justice, legal or not, and most likely violent. Not until I began exploring the files on Mount Olive and Covington County did I see how the struggles that seemed so distant in my childhood were played out on the very landscape that I thought protected me from them. The culture that produced its own spy agency was revealed to me in painful detail. And the parents whom I thought of as not fully engaged in the battle for Civil Rights were fighting the good fight every day and being watched for doing that. The charmed life my parents had constructed for me now stood in sharp contrast to the stories I began to encounter, yet I clung to its memory more tightly than ever.

Before the disquieting discovery of my parents' names in the files, I never knew the fragility of the wall of security created by my parents. Nor did I realize how strong the wall must have been to keep out all that was now before me. As I paged through document after document in the Sovereignty Commission files, I was faced with startling information on my parents and their friends. There was much in the files that was not directly related to my family, but what I found helped me understand why my parents had to be so tight-lipped about my mother's background. The files also held gripping and trivial stories that served as a window into a side of white Mississippi I had never seen before, particularly propaganda circulated among whites to create a group-think mentality about race and segregation. This side of Mississippi was so obsessed with race and "race mixing" that it would dispatch a state investigator to determine the racial identity of a newborn baby.

What was this hydra-headed monster that kept watch over my Mississippi childhood? The Mississippi State Sovereignty Commission was established by an act of the Mississippi legislature on March 29, 1956, an outgrowth of a program then-governor James P. Coleman developed with a state legislative group that had been working to strengthen Mississippi's fortress of racial segregation. This program had seven proposals, one of those being "To create a permanent authority for maintenance of racial segregation with a full staff and funds for its operation to come out of tax money." Upon acceptance and passage of the proposal, the legislative group was then replaced by the Sovereignty Commission, which began a statewide program to promote racial conformity among both black and white citizens.

In 1956, weeks before the establishment of the Sovereignty Commission, Mississippi repealed its compulsory school attendance laws, just in case there was "illegal encroachment" of the federal government to make them integrate public schools. The state couldn't integrate schools its young citizens weren't required to attend by law. The state legislature then took all of this a step further, establishing a group that was legally entitled to do anything necessary to maintain segregation, even invading the privacy of its citizens. Yet the carefully crafted language that established the commission did not use the words segregation or integration:

> It shall be the duty of the commission to do and perform any and all acts and things deemed necessary and proper to protect the sovereignty of the State of Mississippi, and her sister states, from encroachment thereon by the Federal Government . . . and to resist the usurpation of the rights and powers reserved to this state and our sister states by the Federal Government or any branch, department or agency thereof.

During my investigation of the Sovereignty Commission files, the doublespeak and coded speech of the charter and similar treatises served as a continuous source of amusement. I read the Commission's charter over and over again trying to figure out what it meant and how such an obtusely worded law could lead to spying and invasion of privacy. From what I could tell, "encroachment" was used as a substitute for "forced racial integration." The use of the word "sovereignty" was a crafty sophisticated way of expressing the state of Mississippi's resolve to preserve and protect racial segregation and prevent outsiders from changing Mississippi's segregationist way of life. Dating back to before the Civil War, Mississippi proclaimed its "sovereignty" under the guise of states' rights as a means of maintaining a status quo acceptable to its white citizens.

But how did all of this evolve into a state-run spy network? In looking through material from the early years of the Sovereignty Commission, I discovered that the Commission's work began largely as a nationwide public relations campaign to show the benefits of segregation. As time went on, Commission members realized that the public relations efforts were not working to stop the forces of integration outside of Mississippi. In fact, they sensed that the Civil Rights movement would reach Mississippi somehow, someway, and the state's power structure had to find a way to stop that from happening. Quickly, the work of the Sovereignty Commission evolved into defending state-sanctioned racism as well as initiating investigations into anyone or any force that got in the way of perpetuating the established racial status quo. If the war against integration could not be won outside of Mississippi, it would be fought with a calculated winning strategy within the state's borders, among the people who could be influenced the most by pressure and intimidation.

The Sovereignty Commission's influence began at the top of state government. It had its offices in the state capitol, a floor above the governor, and like any other government bureau was staffed by men and women paid by Mississippi taxpayers' dollars. The governor, ex officio, served as the chairman of the Sovereignty Commission and sat on its board. The lieutenant governor was the vice chairman. The state attorney general, the speaker of the legislature, as well as various legislators and noted lawyers held seats on the Commission. By the time it closed in 1973, the Commission's investigators secured confidential files on 87,000 people, making it the largest state-level spying effort in U.S. history.

In its early days, much of the work of the Commission consisted of developing propaganda films and pamphlets targeted at Northern reporters who covered the state to accept Mississippi's stand on racial issues. The Sovereignty Commission proclaimed that the main objective of the films and public relations was to prove that segregation is best "for the dignity and progress of both races." In the files I found draft scripts for films that included scenes of black schools deemed to be comparable to white schools in the same community. The scriptwriter's notes state that the purpose of this scene is to show that "both races are happier and can make greater progress in their own schools." To that end, the final film, *The Message from Mississippi,* which was sent to media and civic groups all across the country, included a message from Governor Ross Barnett proclaiming that black Mississippians preferred the state's segregated way of life. The film featured black leaders sympathetic to the cause of segregation as well as white leaders.

Pamphlets were a more popular form of spreading the Sovereignty Commission's message from the top of state government to the white citizenry in small towns around the state. They were even mailed outside of Mississippi, to groups the state wanted to lobby should it ever need them to defend the segregationist policy of the state. One of the Commission's early pamphlets was entitled "Don't Stone Her Until You Hear Her Side." Its front cover bore a caricature of a white woman—a symbol of Mississippi—who is being stoned by three white men representing agitators from the North. Seven thousand copies of the pamphlet were mailed to targeted Northern newspapers, radio, and television stations to propagate Mississippi's position on segregation and race relations.

The Sovereignty Commission even ran a speaker's bureau that sent Mississippians, including the governor's cousin, to make speeches describing the merits of a segregated society to civic organizations in Northern cities and towns. As with any totalitarian organization, the Commission tightly controlled its message with a list of questions asked and answers given during these speeches, ensuring a consistent party line. In one question-and-answer session, when asked if Mississippi's black population preferred segregation, the speaker noted, "We maintain that Negroes like segregation." The speaker elaborated, "There is no law in Mississippi requiring segregation of churches, but neither side is trying to force its way into worship with each other." Even if an answer a speaker gave may have made him appear foolish, speakers were never to question Mississippi's segregation laws.

By the 1960s, under the solidly segregationist Governor Ross Barnett, the Sovereignty Commission became less of a propaganda and public relations agency and more like the secret police agency of a totalitarian state. Clearly, the public relations campaign had not had the desired impact of protecting Mississippi from "encroachment" by the Federal government. And as the Civil Rights movement gained more momentum, the social and political atmosphere of conformity, intolerance, and repression became even stronger in Mississippi. As a result, the language establishing the Sovereignty Commission came to be interpreted more broadly: The state legislature decided that anyone or any organization that had anything to do with black Mississippians' Civil Rights struggles was subversive and thus a threat to state sovereignty. And if you were a subversive, you had to be a communist, for Mississippi's whole fight against the Civil Rights movement was predicated on the position that the demand by its black citizens to dismantle Jim Crow segregation was all a communist plot. The spirit of McCarthyism, though fading in the rest of the country, was alive and well in 1960s Mississippi.

This propaganda that black Mississippians who fought for civil rights were communists quickly became accepted as fact, largely due to campaigns by the Citizens' Council, as well as misinformation spread by Sovereignty Commission informants. Informants sometimes deceptively reported the presence of communist party materials among movement leaders merely to demonstrate their value as informants and not based on credible evidence. Mississippi politicians and the Citizens' Council used the communist label to undermine the credibility of the people who were involved in civil rights activities in the state. Of course, the vast majority of civil rights leaders were not associated with any communist organizations. But as former Sovereignty Commissioner Michael Smith later put it, "if you travel in the company of a skunk, you're going to smell like a skunk."

With this wrongful assumption coming into favor, the Sovereignty Commission initiated a search for any evidence that could possibly connect the "world Communist conspiracy" with the civil rights movement in Mississippi. To root out black communist subversives, Mississippi's State Sovereignty Commission and its staff of attorneys and former McCarthy-era FBI agents then launched in March 1961 a detailed investigative program to compile files on individuals whose "utterances or actions indicate that they should be watched with suspicion on future racial attitudes." However, before this program had even begun, as a pre-emptive strike the Sovereignty Commission initiated 230 investigations covering all of Mississippi's 82 counties. A full-blown CIA-like operation had begun.

It was during this series of investigations that my parents' names were entered in the files of those whose utterances and actions should be watched.

Months went by after that evening in 1998 in my house in Washington, D.C., when I discovered my parents' names in the Sovereignty Commission files before I could muster up the courage to go and search through those documents. I was truly afraid of what might be lurking in their contents. The physical remains of my early life were gone: the old home place, Lincoln School, many of the people themselves. All I had left were cherished recollections of places, people, and childhood that I had reconstructed to comfort me. Would I dare spoil the memories by what I might find in the Sovereignty Commission files? I even asked myself how I could reconcile these two worlds, one I loved and one I looked upon with disgust. I resolved that I wanted to judge what was true about the past.

Only then could I bring my two views of Mississippi together: the terror and the magnificence.

Before I went to Mississippi, I sent away for the documents that bore my parents' names. The file that arrived in my mailbox a month later seemed relatively innocuous: a list of names. However, my parents were not on the same list. Why this happened wasn't clear to me from the material I had received, which left me with the same puzzlement I felt looking at the ACLU website.

Something told me that there was more behind these papers. Exactly how had my parents landed on separate lists? I had to know. On a fall morning in 1999, I pulled out of my driveway in Washington, D.C., and drove straight to Mississippi to find out why. The next morning, after I walked past the Confederate memorial and up the marble steps into the reading room of the Mississippi Department of Archives and History in Jackson, I spent hours looking at page after page of documents on a computer screen. With blind determination, day after day I searched vigorously to find out why my family was worthy of being watched by the state of Mississippi. This search led to a frustrating series of researcher's dead ends and wrong turns. I searched by name, county, town, and even categories such as "integration agitators." What I discovered during the course of these twists and turns was that parts of the files are closed for reasons of privacy rights. Within the vast files, material exists that I might have found to be personally enlightening, but the main subject of the file has chosen to keep his or her file sealed.

After the first day, I felt like a stranger lost on an unfamiliar rambling country road, since each document I called up on the archive's Hewlett-Packard computer sent me in an unexpected direction. Once I learned the ropes, the files became an obsession. I combed the disembodied documents not just for my family's connections to the files, but also for random hideous insights about complete strangers whose lives had been disrupted and sometimes destroyed by the Commission's investigations. One file detailed the framing of a black man by the name of Clyde Kennard for allegedly stealing $25 worth of chicken feed, just so that he could be jailed and would no longer strive to gain admission to the University of Southern Mississippi. In that report, I also learned that an associate of my father's, a man who on occasion was a guest in our home, was a party to this framing.

This file was one of the most painful to read, and not just because of the personal tie, which was mildly jarring. On each progressive document, the lies and racial hate were like nothing I had ever seen before. The story grew more heartbreaking on each successive page. As I read on, I learned that Kennard's health began to fail: Two years into his seven-year jail sentence for the crime he did not commit, doctors found that Kennard had intestinal cancer. Governor Barnett ignored recommendations to release him for health reasons, relenting a year later when he realized that Mississippi would get unfavorable publicity if Clyde Kennard died in prison. Only months after his release, Clyde Kennard died in a Chicago hospital on the Fourth of July, 1963, at the age of thirty-six.

Another voluminous file told the story of two boys, aged eight and nine, who had never attended school a day in their lives because they were believed to be 1/16 or 1/32 Negro, and neither the black nor the white school system would accept them. Their plight became wrenching to me when I located their photographs and saw that their skin tone was close to that of my own sons, who happened to be the same ages at the time. Like my own mother, these two boys had birth certificates certifying them as white. But unlike my mother, their racial designation moved from being a personal affair to one that was sent to the governor of the state for resolution.

Other files revealed letters from the Commission's paid informants, largely African-American, offering their services to spy on NAACP and voter registration meetings for a fee, of course. One of the African-American informants was enlisted to keep an eye on Medgar Evers as early as 1958, which was when the Commission compiled a six-page memo entitled "Medgar Evers—Integration Agitator." In another file I read about a Catholic priest who had been visited by a Sovereignty Commission investigator just for allowing a black woman to attend Sunday mass. It took a threat of excommunication to the parishioner who turned the priest in to get the investigator to back down. After a closer look at the file, I soon realized that the players in this petty drama were people I knew, or at least thought I knew.

It did not take long to realize that a methodical approach to finding information in the files was only one research strategy. The Commission's investigations were serendipitous in their approach and subject, based more on whim than sound evidence, and my strategy for finding specific information in the records had to take on similar characteristics. I threw my list of names and notes out the window and began to wander from subject to subject seeing what I might find.

Because of my obsession with finding connections in the files, I was often the first to arrive in the reading room and the last to leave. Hours passed quickly and relatively unnoticed as I sat at the computer and clicked through file after file for connections between the disparate documents I found and my early memories. The tone of some of the documents projected on the computer screen turned sinister, while others were actually comical. The Sovereignty Commission once sent an investigator to examine a newborn baby's fingernails and the ends of its fingers to determine whether the child was part black. "We both agreed," said the Commission's investigator, "We were not qualified to say it was a part Negro child, but we could say it was not 100 percent Caucasian." But like the missing pieces of a puzzle, some parts finally came together to make the picture complete; others prompted still more questions. I was beginning to see vividly the side of Mississippi that I had seen only in brief glimpses as a child and had allowed nostalgia to distort in the years intervening.

In many of the files, names of familiar people and places turned up, some of them the same people who had welcomed me as a child on their farms and into their living rooms, such as Mr. Rutland, the highway patrolman who sometimes quail-hunted with my father. According to the files, it appeared that

Mr. Rutland was accused, seemingly for political reasons, of helping blacks to register to vote. Though nothing made the connection clear, I couldn't help but wonder if his close relationship with my family had something to do with this accusation. But again, the trail ended with this report, which was dated July 1962, a time when the Sovereignty Commission clearly had bigger fish to fry with a more active voter registration movement in nearby McComb, led by Student Nonviolent Coordinating Committee leader Bob Moses.

Other connections I made had much more personal impact. I knew the players, like the local sheriff, and had witnessed my father having a conversation with him on a trip to town in Mount Olive or in neighboring Collins. In my childlike innocence I thought the sheriff was there to help. It seemed that Mount Olive and Covington County were no different from other parts of Mississippi, though: The sheriff regularly offered his cooperation to the Sovereignty Commission and maintained two black informants, whose identities were masked but who seemed familiar to me nonetheless. I wondered then and became convinced that the man who accused Mr. Rutland of registering blacks to vote gave me a lollypop each time I visited his store. The past was now laid out before me, at least partially; it was now up to me to align my perception of it with the realities.

This was one of the first documents I read:

The names included in this file are not intended to represent every individual Negro in Mississippi

who belongs or is sympathetic to the NAACP.
However, these names are of those individuals who
have shown up constantly in our continuing investigations as being active in their support of the
NAACP across the state.

This list is not meant to be a static list since
changes are constantly necessary as new names are
added, and some very few of those already included become disillusioned with the NAACP
drop their memberships and get in step with the
majority of Negroes in the State. When this happens, we remove their names from the list.

This statement preceded a list of names in the files of the
Mississippi State Sovereignty Commission that included a list
of license plates of attendees of NAACP meetings across the
state. Although this document was linked to my father's name
in the index, his name was not on the license plate list. Initially, I thought the reason my father and mother were among
the 87,000 names in the files was on account of their work with
the local NAACP's voter registration efforts, including tips on
passing the literacy test. They contributed regularly to a fund
that paid poll taxes for those who could not afford to pay them;
one of them, and often both, attended every NAACP meeting.
Yet when I paged through the document, I did not find the
name Warren or Lucille Eubanks. I did find the name of Boyd
Noffett of Mount Olive, a name I did not recognize. After calling my mother and prodding old family friends to find out who

this person was, no one could tell me anything, not even the former president of Covington County's NAACP. My best guess was that this Boyd Noffett was a code name or a poor transcription from the records; maybe it was even a code name for my father. This was my first encounter with the haphazard, keystone cops nature of some of the information in the files. Although the Sovereignty Commission quietly dispersed its eyes and ears throughout the state to crush the Civil Rights crusades, it did not see or hear clearly. And often, it saw only what it wanted to see, or whatever juicy tidbits or lies their informants could string along for them to keep informant's fees coming each month.

If my parents weren't targeted for being NAACP members, I thought, why were they in the files at all? Wasn't the Sovereignty Commission just targeting activists, agitators, and subversives?

Although the Sovereignty Commission sought to flush out any group it deemed subversive, after paging through the files I realized that almost anything you did in Mississippi in the mid-1950s up though the early 1970s might land your name on a list of "suspicious" people to be watched. The reason was tied directly to the circumstances that led my parents to leave the Mississippi Delta: In the wake of the Supreme Court's *Brown* v. *Board of Education* case, Mississippi's ruling political class chose to make its already closed society even more self-contained. Any cultural, social, or political influence that came from outside of the confines of Mississippi's borders was unwelcome and suspect. Perhaps because the state's cultural identity was so closely linked with the segregated way of life, Mississippi's white citizens set up white supremacist groups like the Citizens' Council, commonly known as "the uptown Klan," all across the state to organize against integration and black civil rights. The Citizens' Council received funds from the Sovereignty Commission, which served as a funnel for tax dollars to support its activities. The Citizens' Council also served as the impetus for many of the Sovereignty Commission's investigations, including those in Covington County, which I discovered was one of the first counties in the state to organize a Citizens' Council.

On February 11, 1959, a memorandum with the subject "NAACP, Collins, Mississippi" was issued to the director of the State Sovereignty Commission:

> Sheriff Dale Shoemake advised that, although he could not put his finger on any NAACP member in his county, he was of the opinion that there were a number of NAACP members who were acting in a very quiet manner in Covington County. He advised that due to unscrupulous activities of certain politicians, such as Supt. of Education Ellis Flynt and the Circuit Clerk Travis Aultman, that approximately 800 Negroes had been registered to vote in Covington County.

The NAACP members acting in a very quiet manner were my father and his associate Andrew Reeves. At the time, the

NAACP in Covington County was operating under an assumed name: The Benevolent Brotherhood Association of Covington County. A benign organizational designation such as this escaped the notice of the Sovereignty Commission and made its activities less noticeable too. So the description is accurate: The NAACP was acting "in a very quiet manner." My father and Mr. Reeves, both of whom were among those blacks who were registered to vote, knew Sheriff Shoemake would be watching them. That was just a given in small towns all across Mississippi. But they didn't think the state of Mississippi would be monitoring their activities as well.

This document also reveals one of the major problems about the information in the file. Some of it is unreliable or inflated; some of it is outright lies and untruths. In 1959, Covington County records show only around 500 blacks registered to vote, not the 800 blacks that the sheriff claims. In many Sovereignty Commission investigations the truth was stretched and manipulated, just as it would be in the communist states for which white Mississippians voiced their disdain and believed influenced its Negroes to demand their civil rights. After looking at some related documents it became clear that Sheriff Shoemake was attempting to use the state-run spy agency for his personal political gain, as a tool for garnering support for his re-election bid. Though I did not run across another case in the files where the Sovereignty Commission and its agents were manipulated for political gain, I am certain it was a popular ploy.

Since the effort to root out the NAACP in Covington County and a few other parts of Mississippi was unsuccessful, the Commission chose another tactic. In the continuing effort to identify NAACP members, stop voter registration, and discover the identity of subversives, the director of the Sovereignty Commission decided that the names of all black teachers should be kept in their files. Teachers were the largest group of professional blacks in the state, and the Sovereignty Commission saw them as prime targets to be influenced by the young Civil Rights workers who were organizing black Mississippians in the movement. So, in a February 1962 memo, the director of the Sovereignty Commission issued a directive to secure a list of names of teachers in Covington County, as well as in five other neighboring counties. The directive stated "[In] Any county seat that may have a school operated by the municipality, contact the Superintendents of city schools in order to secure the names of the colored teachers." This effort was part of the Commission's larger effort to compile files on individuals whose actions, or public utterances, indicated that they should be watched with suspicion for being a subversive or an agitator, whether they were an agitator from Mississippi or an outside agitator.

It was this initiative to build up the files on subversives that landed my mother's name in the files. Because teachers had signed a loyalty oath to the state of Mississippi, promising to uphold the laws of the state and to list their membership in any organizations outside of their work for the state, any Civil Rights activity qualified as a violation of that oath. Once the names of the black teachers and administrators were collected on a list, the Sovereignty Commission built specifically indexed files to cross-check that list against any name that turned up in the files they maintained in any of thirteen subject categories. Those categories included groups deemed undesirable by the state: race agitators, integration organizations, school integration, civil rights-elections, civil rights-violence, and miscellaneous inquiry. The Sovereignty Commission kept thousands of index cards of names, with cross references to investigative reports that would help its staff to identify anyone who did not conform with its point of view. Once your name turned up on one of the lists of unapproved activities or categories, you could be reported to your employer or local law enforcement authorities. If you were a state employee, like a teacher, you could lose your job, as well as find yourself at the mercy of Mississippi's local criminal justice system. Either way, the outcome of turning up on the wrong Sovereignty Commission list could place you and your family in personal danger, since the whole idea was to keep track of who should be watched, monitor what they were doing, and then decide whether they should be continued to be watched or turned over to local authorities.

The investigations of black schoolteachers received the cooperation of the superintendent of education of Covington County, Denson Lott. He told Sovereignty Commission investigator Andy Hopkins that as far as he knew neither "the NAACP nor any other subversive organization is causing any trouble in any of the schools in Covington County at this time" and that he was under the impression that "the Negroes were well satisfied with school facilities of Covington County." Lott further assisted the Commission by promoting a propaganda piece for separate-but-equal education called "Mississippi's Great School Program" that featured Carver School, which was under his supervision.

The investigation report on Denson Lott and his cooperation with the Sovereignty Commission to put the name of my mother and her fellow teachers in the files led me to do a search on his name in the files. I stared in shock at the screen when his named turned up in a file labeled "White Knights of the Ku Klux Klan." The next thing I knew I was reading a February 1966 article from the *Jackson Daily News* with the headline "Mississippi's Klan: Report Named A Lot of Names." In the article was a list of names of people identified by the FBI and the House Un-American Activities Committee as associated with the White Knights of the Ku Klux Klan. Denson "Pee Wee" Lott was on the list, as the head of the Klavern for Covington County. Because the list appeared in the Hederman-owned *Jackson Daily News*, which often censored such reports, it appeared with the following editor's note and caveat: "Any facts presented in the following articles were taken directly from the volumes of HUAC reports." Although this was front-page news, the Hederman organization wanted to make clear that it had not collected the facts contained in the article.

So, not only were my mother and her co-workers on the list of people to be watched, but they had been put on the list by a Klansman, who, it seemed, was an officer of the Klan as well. When Lott promised to cooperate with the Commission "should the NAACP attempt to create trouble in the schools of his county," was he doing it as superintendent of education or as part of his duties as a Klan officer? I could only stare at the screen and wonder about what went through Denson Lott's mind at that time.

Unlike my mother, my father had a direct route into the Sovereignty Commission files that did not involve an officer of the Klan. His entry into the files came at the direct initiation of the governor, Ross Barnett. On December 9, 1960, Janie L. Brewer of Shubuta, Mississippi, wrote to Governor Ross Barnett about her shock and dismay that a Negro home agent was present at a monthly meeting of the Clarke County Monthly Home Demonstration Leaders: "I feel it is my duty as a citizen too *(sic)* cooperate in at least postponing integration, and I know you do. I feel you will look into what is happening in Home Demonstration Clubs over the state." Although the governor did not look into the situation directly, he sent a personal memo to the Sovereignty Commission ordering an investigation. In keeping with its mission to make white citizens feel secure from encroachment from integration or integrationists, the Sovereignty Commission was authorized to investigate any person or organization at the behest of any private white citizen of the state. The subject of this particular investigation: NAACP or other subversive activities in Clarke County and Jasper County.

What the investigator found was that an integrated meeting had taken place and that other integrated activities were taking place under the auspices of county agents and home agents across the state, including my father. As a preschool-age boy, I had sat quietly in the background at some of the same meetings mentioned in the report. Suspecting the influence of the

NAACP, the Sovereignty Commission investigator decided that the names of all county agents and home agents, white and black, should be placed in a dossier for reference should any other similar incidents occur. In addition, to monitor the influence of the NAACP, the lists were then cross-checked with the index file the Commission maintained.

On the surface, having one's name on a list in a file of a vast bureaucratic agency does not seem like a threat to personal freedom, nor does it seem as if it could endanger your life. But in the 1960s in Mississippi, fear and suspicion held such a stranglehold on the white power structure of the state that even insignificant steps across the line of Jim Crow might put you or your family in jeopardy. Once you were in the Sovereignty Commission files, a simple twist of fate could turn a simple name on a list into a victim of the Commission's persecution.

Besides gathering information, the Sovereignty Commission also pointed fingers at those it felt were guilty of trying to change the Mississippi way of life. "Our investigations indicate that three of your employees are very active in the NAACP and another employee suspected of similar work," states a 1964 letter from the commission director to the personnel manager of Jackson Title Company.

The Commission is even linked to some of the most notorious crimes committed in the Civil Rights era, including the murders of Michael Schwerner, James Chaney, and Andrew Goodman. Michael Schwerner's physical description, birthday, address, and telephone number were all collected by the Sovereignty Commission. In 1964, an informant provided the Commission with the license plate number of his Ford station wagon. According to Sovereignty Commission records, all of this information was shared with law enforcement officers in and around Neshoba County, and even the Citizens' Council, creating an atmosphere that encouraged people to take the law into their own hands. Though the Sovereignty Commission was not directly involved, the files reveal that the information provided by the Sovereignty Commission was used by the people who wanted to harm Schwerner and his fellow Civil Rights workers and eventually killed them.

Had the license plate of my family's car turned up on a similar list, my whole family could have been murdered. Since my parents were not Civil Rights activists, the chances were slim that my family would ever have been hunted down. However, an undated speech by Sovereignty Commission director Earle Johnston, Jr., made me think otherwise:

> We made investigations, and when information is accumulated which may be of value to a city or a group, we refer it to those people with a recommendation to help avoid a critical situation. We are very proud that many times our efforts have been most effective.
>
> Of course, we have had incidents in Mississippi and we will continue to have incidents. The Public Health Service has never been able to eradicate illness through preventive medicine. When Illness occurs, you must call your doctor. When some of

our projects fail and incidents result, you must call
in your law enforcement officials.

After reading that statement, one thing became clear: The
Sovereignty Commission was determined to cast the widest net
possible to maintain segregation. From high-profile Civil
Rights workers to law-abiding local people who were perceived
as agitators, the idea was to eradicate any person who challenged the segregated system in Mississippi.

The following entry in the Sovereignty Commission file was
yet another look-see into its effort to offer "the services of the
Sovereignty Commission in all integration matters":

> I did however contact Mr. Sam Graham, Sheriff of
> Covington County. He stated he had a report that
> Negroes might try to integrate Mike Connor
> Memorial Park Lake. There were four Negroes that
> were sold a permit by the Game and Fish Commis-
> sion but they fished early and left when the boats
> started in. Other than that, there is no race problem
> here. Other than that, there is no race problems
> here. The only Negro that the Sheriff knows could
> possibly be an agitator is a Negro preacher in the
> Hopewell Community. The Sheriff has a couple of
> old reliable Negro informers in Covington County
> who will keep him informed if anything develops.

When I was a boy, I spent quiet summer afternoons fishing
with my father at Mike Connor Lake. Although we always kept

to the "colored" side of the lake, after reading this file entry I realized our very presence there, just a father and son out together fishing, could be viewed as a subversive activity in Mississippi in the 1960s. Those lines disturbed what was once a peaceful memory of a beautiful, seemingly tranquil place. Though the memory lingers, it is tarnished forever.

The sheriff had his own set of Negro informers in the county. I sat before the computer in the reading room wondering who these people were. Was it someone my family knew? I was certain it was.

Up until this moment, nothing had turned up in the files of Covington County mentioning black informants to the Sovereignty Commission. The spies had been white former FBI agents or people like the superintendent of education who were the eyes and ears of the Commission. But throughout the state, the Sovereignty Commission cultivated informants among "a large number of fine, level-headed Negro citizens" who were of the mind that "the best interest of the Negro race lies along segregated paths." Most of these paid and unpaid informants were concentrated in the Mississippi Delta. "They have played no small part in helping maintain the status quo of the races," a Commission document said of its black informants, "[and] [t]his problem will never be resolved without the help and cooperation of the Negroes in the State of Mississippi."

A siege mentality had taken hold of Mississippi, so informants both black and white made the Commission's members investigate anything and everything that might smell of integration, even something so trivial as a black man fishing in a public park on land normally reserved for the white man. Many of the informants only provided the commission with a hodgepodge of rumors and bizarre details, which helped feed hysteria and paranoia. That was certainly the case here. Still, I wanted to know who would lower himself to be a party to spreading rumors in my town. In particular, I wanted to know the black man who would do it. There were no clues in the files about the identity of Covington County's black informant, so I set off to talk with old friends in Mount Olive to see what I could find. It's hard to keep a secret in a small town.

Each person I spoke with pointed to two people: the father and grandfather of a high-school friend, one who had struggled with me through the early days of integration in Mount Olive. Both were regular informants to the sheriff; the sheriff, in turn, relayed everything, no matter how slight, to the Sovereignty Commission. Later, when schools integrated, which the files reveal as marking the end to Sovereignty Commission investigations in and around Mount Olive, according to my old friends one of these men continued to feed information to the sheriff.

And although I had promised myself not to skip any of the pages this time around, this one I chose not to view. I pondered what I would gain by dragging this up with my high-school classmate. What would he gain? I thought about the hate and animosity the Sovereignty Commission had created and decided that to pull those same forces forward forty years served no real purpose. Still, something nagged at me.

What I had come back to Mississippi to do was to understand what really happened in my early days when I was nestled securely on my farm. And I wanted to remain on that course. I decided to dig deeper, but in my own backyard. There was a lot there still unresolved. The files related to school integration nagged at me, more so than what an informant had done for an unknown motive. Reading all of the material in the files pushed forward in my consciousness the time when I first encountered the mindset of the Sovereignty Commission, although then I didn't even realize it. I was becoming a young man in a newly integrated Mississippi, and the years ranged from eighth grade to the end of high school.

Up until this point, the files helped me fill in the gaps in my early childhood memories, to examine a world that I both shut out and was shuttered away from. Now, I had to reach back into a time in my life that I largely chose to forget.

SIX

"Ever Is a Long Time"

On June 23, 1957, a year after the establishment of the Sovereignty Commission and two days before I was born, Mississippi's governor, James P. Coleman, appeared on NBC's "Meet the Press" and was asked whether the public schools in Mississippi would ever be integrated. "Well, ever is a long time," he replied, "[but] I would say that a baby born in Mississippi today will never live long enough to see an integrated school."

My mother quoted those words to my sisters and me as she drove the four of us to our first day at an integrated school. The ride was largely silent, for none of us knew what to expect on that cold January day in 1970. It seemed as if we had been in the car for hours when we turned the corner at Main Street to drive to the front of the school, where we were to be dropped off. Outside Mount Olive School, a dark brownish-black and conspicuously aging brick structure, stood a small group of churlish protesters brandishing brooms and mops threatening to clean black children out of the school like pieces of trash. The memory of the shouts and hate-filled glances of those protesters is one I have resented over the years. But that memory is my personal witness to the last days of segregation in Mississippi.

As we all looked at the school and the protesters, my sister, Gretta, entering the last semester of her senior year, remarked "this place looks like a prison." Her remark proved to be prescient, for soon Mount Olive School began to feel more like a correctional facility and less like an educational institution. On the first day we all received a legal-sized sheet listing the new dress and behavior code, providing rules for the length of boys' hair, girls' skirts, and what constituted appropriate interactions between the sexes. In this strict, artificially structured environment, the three oldest Eubanks children all behaved like inmates, dutifully doing time until a high-school diploma liberated us. And one by one, we turned away from our hometown and Mississippi.

Although Governor Coleman's prediction proved wrong that January day, the protestors served as a chilling testament to how strongly white Mississippians had embraced his sentiments and those of the other segregationist governors who succeeded him over the years. Their rage sprang from the sensibilities of groups such as the Sovereignty Commission and Mississippi White Citizens' Council, two organizations that were inexorably tied together to fight against integration and penetrate Mississippi's cultural mindset. For years, the Citizens' Council distributed prosegregation literature to adults and children alike. One manual distributed to white public-school children included this lesson: "God wanted the white

"Mount Olive is a place where nothing ever happens," I said as a child. In 2003, as pictured here, Mount Olive's tree-lined Main Street projects that description, for the town is as empty as it appears. Though it looks much as I remember it as a child, several businesses have closed and its streets no longer fill with shoppers on a Saturday afternoon.

This house and its setting on a lush, green 80 acres of south Mississippi farmland no longer survives, but it lives on in memory. The house was the core of the Eubanks family farm, the place that protected one family from the turmoil that was Mississippi in the 1960s. It stood just two miles from this sign directing travelers to Mount Olive or Hot Coffee. After destruction by a tornado, all that remains are remnants of the house's foundation.

Me with my dog Blondie, who had a talent for chasing low-flying aircraft, not trucks.

My paternal grandfather, William Frederick Douglas Eubanks, around 1915.

My maternal grandfather, James Morgan Richardson, around 1920.

(left) My father, Warren Ralph Eubanks, as he entered the Army in 1942 at the age of eighteen. (right) My mother, Lucille Edna Eubanks, also at age 18, as she would have looked when she met my father at Tuskegee Institute in 1947.

My parents in Prestwick, Alabama, on their wedding day in 1952. Shortly thereafter, my parents moved to the Mississippi Delta.

Though I only remember seeing markers denoting white or colored only on visits to nearby Jackson or Hattiesburg, these signs, photographed in 1952 for *LOOK* magazine, were a familiar sight in Mississippi and across the south. They served not only to separate the races, but also to perpetuate a culture rooted in white superiority. (photo by John Vachon, *LOOK* Magazine Collection, Prints and Photographs Division, Library of Congress)

Mississippi Gov. James P. Coleman in 1957 as he appeared before the Senate Constitutional Rights Subcommittee. In June of that same year he would appear on NBC's "Meet the Press." When asked whether public schools in Mississippi would ever be integrated, he responded by saying, "Well, ever is a long time. I would say that a baby born in Mississippi today will never live long enough to see an integrated school." (Prints and Photographs Division, Library of Congress)

The Woolworth's lunch counter sit-in in Jackson, May 28, 1963. When I saw this photograph at the age of six, I had no idea what this event meant or what effect it would have on my life. (Fred Blackwell/*The Jackson Daily News*)

Four children sheltered from the world of sit-ins, marches, and threats of violence: Ralph, Sharon, Gretta, and Sylvia Eubanks on Easter Sunday, 1967.

With my father on my tenth birthday. My father, the tree, and the house are now all gone, but the memory of that time runs deep and led me to explore the world of Mississippi's Sovereignty Commission.

Ed King (with bandage) and Aaron Henry as they ran for lieutenant governor and governor of Mississippi in 1963 on the Freedom Democratic ticket. King, a native Mississippian, was a subject of Sovereignty Commission investigations and unsuccessfully fought to maintain individual privacy rights when the files were opened in 1998. (Matt Heron/TakeStock Photography)

On high school graduation day, May 7, 1974, with my favorite teacher, Nell Calhoun. Although she taught math, she fostered in me a lifelong interest in Southern writers, particularly Eudora Welty.

The Mount Olive High School Student Advisory Council of 1971, with me second from left on the front row. Standing to my right is Jim Brewer, who twenty-five years later returned to my side as I examined my conflicted feelings about Mount Olive and the Sovereignty Commission.

A Mississippi Highway Patrolman in September 1962 on the campus of the University of Mississippi as James Meredith tried to register as the first black student there. (© Danny Lyon/Magnum Photos)

James Meredith is escorted by U.S. Marshals at the University of Mississippi, October 1, 1962. In the background is the Lyceum building, the university's main administration building, the scene of rioting the previous evening. (*U.S. News and World Report* Collection, Prints and Photographs Division, Library of Congress).

With fellow winners of the 1974 freshman English Theme Writing Contest at Ole Miss: me, Eileen Shull Staples, and Hardy R. Stone. When asked where to have this photograph taken, I insisted on this spot on the Lyceum steps, near the bullet holes left from the integration of Ole Miss by James Meredith. (University of Mississippi Office of Public Relations)

Ellie J. Dahmer (center), wife of slain Mississippi civil rights worker Vernon Dahmer, Sr., stands on the steps of the Mississippi Department of Archives and History with her son, Vernon, Jr., and daughter, Bettie. In her hands she is holding a package containing the no-longer-secret Sovereignty Commission files relating to her husband's civil rights activities and the aftermath of his firebombing death. After the opening of the files in 1998, this scene was repeated by many Mississippi families who wanted to know what Mississippi's secret files held and led me to check the files on my parents.

U.S. Highway 49 runs through the Mississippi Delta, down to Mount Olive before ending at the Gulf Coast. Over three years, I traversed this entire stretch of U.S. 49, moving from the Delta towns my parents settled in after they married, down to Mount Olive. My sons, Patrick (left) and Aidan (right), also traveled U.S. 49 and other roads like it as we explored Mississippi. Before returning home, we took a break with William Faulkner on Oxford, Mississippi's Courthouse Square. (Photograph on Courthouse Square by James Ronald Bartlett. U.S. Highway 49 © Danny Lyon/Magnum Photos)

people to live alone. And He wanted the colored people to live alone. . . . This is called our Southern Way of Life. Do you know that some people want the Negroes to live with white people? These people want us to be unhappy." It was Governor Coleman who signed the legislation that founded the Sovereignty Commission, which promoted the same philosophy as the Citizens' Council and eventually provided the funding for its books and pamphlets. And Governor Coleman passed this legacy down to his successors, Ross Barnett, Paul B. Johnson, and John Bell Williams, who in turn kept the organization alive until it crumbled.

Hours of poring over Sovereignty Commission documents provided insight into the minds of those protesters. The twin forces of the Sovereignty Commission and the Citizens' Council and their hold on the racial sensibilities of some of the people in my town and all across Mississippi had fueled the resistance of the protesters. For many years, the Sovereignty Commission gave numerous grants of public funds to the Citizens' Councils of Mississippi to promote racial segregation in its statewide "Forum" programs, including $20,000 in 1960. Citizens' Council Forum was a series of fifteen-minute television and five-minute radio programs with conservative Southern politicians and so-called experts discussing topics such as alleged black inferiority, "the worldwide Communist conspiracy" in the Civil Rights movement, and states' rights.

Racism existed without this effort, yet the money helped the Citizens' Councils' message penetrate the state and hold the racial divide widely apart for as long as possible. When asked to justify the use of public funds to promote segregation, Sovereignty Commission Director Albert Jones proclaimed, "We know of no other facility which offers so much for our cause. . . . It [the Citizens' Council] merits the active financial support of all patriotic Mississippians." Obviously, when issues of race were involved, clear reasoning appeared to vanish from the minds of Mississippi's leaders as they struggled desperately to maintain a rigid system of racial conformity. It was this devotion to racial conformity that kept many whites from even imagining a world that was not segregated. This even included some of the best people in my little town of Mount Olive.

But at the time, all I knew was that the rallying cry of "segregation now and forever," which echoed across the South my entire life, was now dying down to a whisper, with federal court orders that demanded the end of dual school systems all across Mississippi. The investigations of the Sovereignty Commission were secret, and I never paid attention to its existence, even the paragraph about it in my Mississippi history textbook, until its files were opened. The marchers of the Citizens for Local Control of Education, who at the time seemed to mock the slogans and the stance of black Civil Rights workers, along with the Sovereignty Commission, were only fighting another one of the last losing battles of Mississippi's second reconstruction.

Some of the protesters outside the school opted to send their children to private academies. Others chose to move their children to schools in Sullivan's Hollow, which had always been and would always remain all white. Still others, like our white neighbors, the Nichols, who had a prominent role in the protest, accepted and embraced integration. Mrs. Nichols actually preferred for her children to have black rather than white teachers. "Those town teachers just don't treat my children right," I heard her say to my mother once, lamenting that her children were treated like poor white trash by white teachers rather than the upstanding citizens they had been led to believe they were by Citizens' Council propaganda. The day Mrs. Nichols came to my mother to lay her burden down before her she was clearly a changed woman.

There were still residents of Mount Olive who never changed and accepted integration; they kept fighting the battle inside the school. Those were the people who acted like prison guards and made black children feel like inmates. Some of those people who refused to let go of the segregated world promised by the Sovereignty Commission and the Citizens' Council were my teachers.

The Sovereignty Commission had its own agents, a network of spies, subpoena power, and the legal authority to keep its records secret all in the interest of maintaining a segregated society in Mississippi, especially in the public schools. Even with all the power they were given and their generous budget of $250,000 per year, a princely sum in impoverished 1960s Mississippi, they couldn't stop integration from coming. By 1967, in the Commission's report on their work since the passage of the Civil Rights Act of 1964, the group even reconciled itself to an advisory role to the state and local groups on "specific problems brought about by federal court orders, laws passed by

Congress, and demands of minority groups." At that point it was clear to the state-sponsored segregation watchdog organization that the end of their era of power was near.

The local anti-integration group, the Citizens for Local Control of Education, conducted a masterful, albeit crude and homemade, public relations campaign, much like those I had read about in the Sovereignty Commission files. There is nothing in the files to show a direct tie to the Sovereignty Commission or the Citizens' Council, yet the signs of its influence are all there. Like the Sovereignty Commission and the Citizens' Council, our local group maintained that segregation was part of "our Southern way of life" that should be preserved. Of course, part of their message was that integration was tied to communism.

So, on January 8, 1970, almost six years after the passage of the Civil Rights Act, after the Sovereignty Commission's struggle to conquer the hearts and minds of Mississippi and a lengthy court battle by the state to fight integration, schools in thirty districts across Mississippi integrated. The move was made in the middle of the school year because the state had resisted so long. Upon announcing the decision, the judge in the case, Griffin Bell, proclaimed in court, "When we say you have to get started immediately, that is what we mean—tomorrow." I was twelve years old, in the eighth grade, and scared to death of what was to come from that proclamation. Almost overnight I was headed for a face-to-face encounter with the Mississippi that until then I had been shielded from by my parents. And as I look back on it now, I wasn't at all prepared for what I was about to face.

On the overcast day in January, my first day at Mount Olive School, the walk up the steps to the schoolhouse door felt endless. My feet seemed to be made of lead. I finally opened the door, and I walked into a hall freshly painted in institutional off-white, with a large trophy case on the left wall and pictures of past graduating classes on the walls around me. The faces in those photographs seemed to stare at me, and I felt like an unwelcome intruder. Their white faces were unfamiliar, for up until then my history in Mount Olive did not include the people on the walls or the place itself. Now I was "over town," in the part of Mount Olive that all of my life had been off limits.

This building, like the town library, had been a place I could never step inside. Up until that day in January, by local custom and Mississippi law, my presence there was even illegal, because I was black and deemed inferior and unworthy to walk the halls. Going anywhere near this building would have generated the same kind of hostility shown by the protesters who marched outside at that very moment.

I don't remember a first-day assembly or any sort of welcome. Students were just registered and moved as efficiently as possible to their respective spots in the school. While my parents had a discussion with the principal in his office, I waited outside the office to go to my classroom. The principal, Mr. Thornton, was white. Mr. Barron, who had dominated my years at Lincoln School, had now been demoted to assistant principal.

What my parents were discussing with Mr. Thornton was which class I would be assigned to: the all-black eighth-grade class from Lincoln that I learned was being kept together that semester or the white class from Mount Olive. Judge Griffin Bell's court order dictated that blacks and whites would go to school not just in the same building, but also in the same classrooms. That didn't happen in Mount Olive. The black school, Lincoln, had been closed in an attempt to satisfy white families who might refuse to send their children to a school that up until that year had been for blacks only. This happened not just in Mount Olive and Covington County, but all over Mississippi. Long-time black principals and administrators were demoted and the schools, some of which had been touted as being equal to white schools in Sovereignty Commission propaganda distributed in the North, were closed because they were deemed by local school boards to be not good enough for white children.

It did not stop there. The closing of black schools wasn't enough. Instead of full integration, as demanded by the court order, segregated classes were maintained. The races merely coexisted under one roof, up through the end of the school year, with plans to move to fully integrated classes in the fall. With the hindsight of more than thirty years, I realized that none of this made logical sense, but there was the desire among parents and teachers to keep classroom continuity for both sets of students and take a measured approach to integration. This helped the whites control the number of students defecting to the fast-growing segregation academies; if blacks and whites were kept effectively segregated and school proceeded with few incidents, white parents who were on the fence about integration might not move to the academies. From the black perspective, this measured approach helped maintain a degree of black control in the schools, which everyone knew would soon be usurped by whites.

Unlike the rest of the black eighth graders in Mount Olive, I had gone to neighboring Carver School rather than to Lincoln. Being the odd boy out, no one had to maintain any continuity for me. I was already out of my old school, which I had attended under the freedom of choice plan, and since freedom of choice in schools was outlawed, by law I now had to go to school in Mount Olive. Rather than putting me with the black kids from Lincoln, kids I had known my entire life, the principal decided to do what he defined as an "experiment": I would go to all-white classes. No sound social reasoning was given for this decision. Maybe the principal thought someone should broach integration, provide an opportunity for some token interaction with a black person, and thus pave the way for the other black students. Under freedom of choice there had been black children who went to Mount Olive; however, most of them had left, feeling unaccepted and isolated in the time before court-ordered desegregation. Perhaps because I was fair skinned, the feeling was that my lack of pigmentation would not be disruptive to the balance of the class. Whatever the reason or lack thereof, I was put into an integrated classroom, as were my two older sisters, and we bore the burden of being both the subjects of an experiment and trailblazers.

In junior high at Mount Olive, all classes, with the exception of history and social studies, were segregated by sex. After my parents emerged from the principal's office, to my surprise I landed in Mrs. Thornton's homeroom with fourteen white boys. Mrs. Thornton, the wife of the school principal, introduced all of them to me: Jim Brewer, who sat on my left, and Ronnie Kimbrough, who sat on my right, nodded politely, as did several of the other boys. After the introductions, Michael Summrall, known as "Curly," rose to his feet with a couple of other boys and proudly pointed to their mothers in the picket line outside. "My mama's waaaay up front!" Curly announced with glee. Mrs. Thornton, her cheeks red with embarrassment, sternly ordered everyone to sit down and move away from the window.

From that moment almost up until the beginning of my senior year, my memory of my time at Mount Olive School fades in and out of clarity. The isolation of that semester and the ones that followed rattled my senses to the point that I felt disconnected to school, my classmates, and to the little town that I thought would nurture me forever. The experiment of being the trailblazer for my class didn't break me, but it didn't instill a great sense of pride either. I merely felt marooned in that classroom. I performed poorly in school, even failing math in the final grading period, a subject that was one of my favorites and that I got consistently good grades in. After that semester, I realized that in time I would have to leave Mount Olive forever. The onset of adolescence may have had something to do with my feelings then, for every teenager feels some sense of alienation. Yet, feeling isolated at school and unwanted in my hometown, and sensing that same feeling of dislocation from the adults around me, both my parents and teachers, made it much worse.

No one in the eighth-grade classroom that January day had treated me harshly. Curly Summrall's outburst was a statement of fact, albeit one designed to make me squirm. Yet I felt the same message from the pictures that seemed to glare down on me when I came in to school: I was an interloper and would never be made to feel a part of this new school, a place that would define my world for the next four and a half years. Whatever identity I had forged up until now would have to be shoved aside; I would have to fit in here, even though it seemed that no one really wanted me.

The culture of manners in Mount Olive prohibited any brash displays of racism, but racism hung heavily in the air nevertheless. There were no social gatherings at school, with the exception of sporting events. School no longer unified the community; it divided it, and mostly along the racial lines and boundaries that had always been established. I could see it; my classmates, both black and white, could certainly see it; but no one would talk about the division that had arisen as a result of what was to be a unifying act. Silently, we remained divided, clinging to our tribes, whether that tribe was in the white community "over town," in The Jungle, The Quarters, or The Bottom, or in the comfort of our own families. Whatever the division, all cowered in fear that we would be accused of being rude for speaking out against divisions that should not matter anymore. Black or white, we had one thing in common: All of us were taught never to be rude.

With my newfound feeling of hopelessness, each day I walked up the steps of that old brick building, engaged myself with the schoolwork at hand, and shut out much of everything else. Even today, walking the halls of Mount Olive School as an adult casts a pall over me. What little I do remember about that time is the randomness of relationships with fellow students and teachers.

Although the subjects were the same, in some of my classes the cultural context was completely foreign to me. I had been taught about the Civil War and its tie to slavery and emancipation; now I was taught about the "War for Southern Independence." Characterizations of slavery seemed to be taken from the pages of *Gone With the Wind*, if they were discussed at all. But the most dramatic change was the watch that was kept over the books students chose to read.

Before school integration, I had been encouraged to read anything I was capable of reading. Now teachers took a sudden interest in what I read not to encourage me, but to determine whether what I read met with their standards and approval. Once I was asked to cover my copy of Hermann Hesse's *Steppenwolf*; a teacher had found it offensive, and an offensive cover must have offensive content.

The conflicts of Harry Heller in *Steppenwolf* seemed to echo mine: I found myself in a place I no longer understood. Even at the age of thirteen I knew that small Mississippi towns rarely embraced new or different ideas; integration had taken years to come about and was being resisted rather than embraced. Already challenged by integration, the schools and their leadership made it clear that the open exchange of ideas and philosophies would not be tolerated.

By my freshman year of high school, my coping mechanisms were beginning to fall in place: I learned where and when to keep ideas and feelings to myself. I even served on the student council that year, which was the only forum where I felt I could openly and honestly express my thoughts. Still, I chose my alliances within the group carefully, aligning myself with black and white students who, like me, were more inclined to academics than sports.

By this time, I was also reunited with the black students in my class, many of whom I had known since first grade. But we were not reunited in all of our classes, since another line was drawn: I was taking college prep classes in math, science, and English and not many of my black classmates were doing that. Fortunately, my best friend from first grade, Marvin Bridges, was with me in those classes and we vowed to support each other for the duration of our high school years. We were aware that we had to take all our science classes from Pernicie Knight, whom everyone, including the principal, knew despised the presence of blacks in the school. My mother had even tangled with Mrs. Knight, calling her to task for her attempts to demoralize my older sister. My father also tried to reason with Mrs. Knight in his calmer style, and walked away from his conversation with her in a rage. Judging from those two encounters, I knew she had it in for me.

A situation like this called for a plan of action. Always the strategist, my sister Sharon devised a plan. If we repeated verbatim lessons from our textbooks and key parts of Mrs. Knight's lectures, she couldn't fail us. So we memorized passages from biology textbooks, used copies of college-level chemistry books to study, and took extensive notes in class. We drilled until midnight many school nights and arose before dawn to drill again. My friend Marvin and I traded notes, and sometimes studied together over the phone. Even though many of the answers on our tests were correct textbook answers, I always got a "C," and more often than not so did Marvin. Only once do I recall making a "B"; and what I remember about getting that grade was the smirk Mrs. Knight gave me when she handed me the paper and said, "it's so good to see that your work is finally improving."

Mrs. Knight was an ardent Baptist and injected her religious sensibilities and scripture into the classroom, particularly in discussions about evolution. The Book of Genesis was even used as a point-counterpoint to our textbook's brief mention of the theory of evolution. In addition to her religious views, she found a way to preach to us about the horrors of communism, which she often mentioned as a force that was causing ruin in our state and country. Even I knew that this was a veiled reference to Civil Rights and integration, as I had often seen them mentioned in the same way on the pages of the Jackson *Clarion-Ledger*.

Mrs. Knight demanded order and conformity in her classroom, and the most undisciplined students managed to march in step with her every demand. A word from scripture might be invoked to bring order to the class, just as it was often used as a deterrent to cheating. Cheating was placed in a biblical context: It was called stealing, not cheating. During a test, if she noticed a student's eye wandering toward another's paper, she would say loudly "Remember that stealing is stealing in the sight of God. And the Bible says 'Thou shalt not steal'!"

After hearing this homily test after test, I grew weary and angry. How could Mrs. Knight have such an ardent disdain for cheating and then cheat me out of the grade I deserved? Wasn't this a violation of the religious principles she so fervently advocated? By the end of my sophomore year, I had had enough. I wouldn't let my parents confront her, for fear of her turning up the heat on her reprisals; I resolved to take the situation into my own hands.

I asked to see her after class to go over a test, which I knew was "B" if not "A" level work. I remember going over the test point by point, showing her where in the textbook I had gotten the answer. I knew the answer was right because I had committed much of the chapter to memory, and the words I had written were the mirror image of the textbook. When she refused to budge, I turned red in the face and lost my tongue.

All of a sudden, I found myself saying, "Mrs. Knight, stealing is stealing in the sight of God. Thou shalt not steal."

As I stared directly into her eyes, I watched Mrs. Knight's face grow red. Quickly she regained her composure and said with a stammer in her voice, "If I change your grade, I'll have to do it for everyone else." Again, I reminded her, this time raising the timbre of my voice: "Stealing is stealing in the sight of God, Mrs. Knight." Then I turned and walked out.

Mrs. Knight and I fought throughout three long years of science classes, plus the entire year that she was the sponsor of my senior class. Math class saved me and my teacher, Mrs. Calhoun, taught me a love for the power of numbers. Her brand of math was not mere equations and calculations; we were taught how mathematical concepts could be applied to logic, clear thinking, and philosophy. Unlike Mrs. Knight, Mrs. Calhoun dared to explore ideas that made her uncomfortable. To settle arguments, she sometimes would compare differing ideas among students using the form of a mathematical proof on the board.

To shut out whatever was going on around me that I didn't want to face, I always had a book to read. I expected that Mrs. Calhoun wanted to censor my reading as well. Why not? My English teacher had tried, and even my fellow students had looked at the books I read with suspicion. But after a few exchanges, I learned that Mrs. Calhoun was actually interested in what I was reading. She might even discuss the book with me. Never did she criticize me for reading something others in Mount Olive thought inappropriate.

Mrs. Calhoun taught math and physics, but her interests were far broader, which I learned when I left my books on the windowsill of her classroom between lunch period and her class. She allowed many of her students to do this to save time on our truncated lunch hour. Lunch times and rules were tightly outlined on our legal-sized list of rules, which my allied members of the student council knew was designed specifically to decrease the social interaction between black and white students. Most days I would leave lunch early to go to Mrs. Calhoun's class, and we would talk about what I was reading rather than the math or physics homework. She encouraged me to read more, particularly Welty and Faulkner, two writers who held no interest for me at the time. I thought I had nothing in common with their white Southern point of view. I had more empathy with the Victorian world depicted by Charles Dickens in *David Copperfield*, an early favorite of mine. But Mrs. Calhoun proved me wrong.

Many of the books she felt I should read, like *As I Lay Dying* and various collections of short stories of Eudora Welty, were what kept me going through high school. Few of my classmates were passionate readers, and those who were leaned more toward Southern writers. My newfound interest in Southern writers gave me something in common with them that my interest in books written by foreigners could not. Mrs. Calhoun had sensed that I had a strong desire to be different from my classmates, but knew that my survival at Mount Olive School depended on finding common ground with those around me. And she taught me how to find that common ground, in between lessons in math, physics, and our one-on-one discussion of literature.

In the early days of integration, common ground between the races increased in importance despite the attempts to keep blacks and whites separated, even when under the roof of the same school. The separation could not be made to last forever. By my freshman year, there were integrated sports teams, bands, and classes. In my sophomore year, you could feel the groups moving together; a winning football season, culminating in a division championship, being the first event that brought real unity. Our marching band, in which I played trumpet, performed a half-time show at the winning game, and I remember it as the first time that black and white students were united as fellow students, a student body, not divided by the color of our skin. That evening we cheered, laughed, and cried together.

On the way home from the game, the band, which was evenly integrated, came together to sing songs at the back of the bus. What actually happened that evening was a sharing of our cultures: white country rock and black soul. We sang the songs each group listened to on late-night clear channel AM radio stations, the white kids teaching the black kids the lyrics to "The Night They Drove Old Dixie Down" and the black kids teaching the whites to sing Curtis Mayfield and the Impressions' song "A Choice of Colors." I'll never forget the sound of our voices:

> If you had a choice of color
> Which one would you choose my brothers?
> If there was no day or night
> Which would you prefer to be right?

It was silent after one lead singer finished. Then we all laughed together and moved on to the next song. Almost two years before that evening, the parents of a couple of the kids singing on the bus that night had been on a picket line to keep kids like us apart. That evening, we wanted to be together. And none of us would have chosen to be different, to be a color different from what we were.

Though the memory of that evening has stayed with me through the years, there were other times as well when the differences between the races didn't matter in Mount Olive. Still, none of those occasions has stayed with me the way that night did.

In the middle of my senior year, my parents moved to North Mississippi to a little town called Houston, where my father was to direct the county's office for the Farmer's Home Administration. He had fought hard for the job, but I didn't want to leave in the middle of my senior year. Finally, high school was fun, and the end was in sight. I was a straight-A student thanks to no classes with Mrs. Knight. I was on a winning streak, one that would help me thumb my nose at her in the process: My grades were going to allow me to graduate with honors. To keep up the momentum I had built, Alice and Julius Magee, my lifelong surrogate grandparents, invited me to live with them.

The senior year is typically a carefree time, and a sense of freedom is what I remember most about that year. But while I had fun, at night in my bed at the Magees' house I thought about what was to come: What would become of our farm, would we ever live there again, could I just leave Mount Olive behind? Did I really want to leave Mississippi? Something told me that I had to, and for a long time something inside me wanted to. There was also so much from high school that I wanted to forget, and I yearned for a place to start over where I could begin to forget.

For all my restless nights, little that I thought about that spring was within my power to change. My father had already begun to build a new life for my family in North Mississippi.

Though I couldn't bring myself to admit it, I had to turn my back on life in Mount Olive too. The night I got my high-school diploma, I left Mount Olive forever.

For years, I corresponded regularly with Mrs. Calhoun, right up until her death, keeping her as my only tie to my time in high school. I carried the note I received from her daughter telling me of her death in my briefcase. "In her last days she spoke of her former students and their achievements often, and she always mentioned you," the note said. Yet when I read that note I didn't think I ever said enough to her about how much she had helped me, although I think she knew. Somehow the anger I felt at Mrs. Knight overshadowed my feelings for Mrs. Calhoun.

Mrs. Knight still lives in Mount Olive, and I thought of her as I paged through document after document of the Sovereignty Commission that equated integration and the Civil Rights movement with communism. One afternoon I sat in the reading room of the archives in Jackson reading a Sovereignty Commission document that called Tougaloo College, a base for the Civil Rights movement in Jackson, a haven for "political agitators and possibly some communists." As I read those words, I heard them in my head spoken by Mrs. Knight. Those very words could have been bandied about in one of her anti-communism rants.

Soon after reading that report on Tougaloo, I drove through Mount Olive and stopped by Mrs. Knight's house. I needed to know if the person who held the beliefs that were written in the report I had just read still harbored those same views. And, most of all, I wanted to know if it was because of these same beliefs that she had treated me the way she did. I parked in front of her house, and I walked to the door. But something kept me from ringing the bell.

As I drove away, I felt like a coward for not confronting her. I also thought that some demons aren't worth wrestling to the ground. This one was best left alone, to be allowed to die quietly, just as the times that created the demons have withered, died, and almost faded away.

SEVEN

Rebel Flags
and Bullet Holes

*F*rom the time I entered high school, I dreamed of leaving small-town Mississippi. My deepest secret desire was to live *anywhere* but Mississippi, particularly somewhere that no one knew anything about me. During my senior year, as I looked for something to fill the void left by my parents' moving away, the dream only grew stronger.

In small towns like Mount Olive, everyone knows you, which is a blessing as a child and a curse as an adolescent. As a teenager, well-meaning family friends monitored my every move; so did people who didn't know me at all. Just before my parents moved, the service station attendant where I gassed up my father's Volkswagen even called his office once to say, "You better tell your boy not to drive around with white girls riding on the front seat of his car." I was not alone with this girl and was in fact accompanied by a white male classmate. We were just a group of teenagers innocently selling ads for "The Pirate," our high school yearbook. Later that night my father talked quietly to me about the incident on our front porch, and I knew then that someway, somehow, I had to leave Mississippi.

I was sixteen years old.

Judging from the pictures in the recruitment material that I kept stashed away in my room, Tulane University was made just for me. New Orleans, I thought, was big enough to have the anonymity I craved, yet still Southern and close enough to home so that I could run back with my tail between my legs if I needed to. I knew that I wouldn't know anyone at Tulane. None of my classmates from Mount Olive were even thinking of applying there. Judging from the recruitment poster that hung in Mrs. Calhoun's classroom, I was the only student to have taken one of the cards to request an application for admission. That was good. I'd get a fresh start and have some fun after enduring four years of Mount Olive High School.

But my father insisted that I stay in Mississippi. I wasn't even allowed to apply to Tulane.

"There's Mississippi Southern, Mississippi State, or Ole Miss. Take your pick," he told me. Lots of people from Mount Olive went to Southern, since Hattiesburg was just half an hour away. My sister Sharon was at Mississippi State; I didn't want to spend the next four years in her shadow. There was no one from my class at Mount Olive going to Ole Miss. I craved independence from my family and wanted to make a break with Mount Olive, so I chose Ole Miss. In spite of its history and its reputation as an unfriendly place for a young black man, Ole Miss seemed to be the only choice I had.

Sensing my need for autonomy, my father supported my decision. He also wanted me to go to medical school and saw an Ole Miss degree as my first step toward that goal. Ever the dutiful son, I went along with this plan. My mother, however, was against my going to Ole Miss. "I can't look at Ole Miss without thinking of the blood flowing down its streets," she proclaimed with a pointed reference to the integration of Ole Miss as well as an air of drama and righteous indignation. Most of all, she worried that I would not be strong enough to make it at Ole Miss. My mother's questioning sealed my decision. It became clear what I would do. By going to Ole Miss, I could satisfy the demands of my father, prove my mother wrong, and cut her apron strings in the process. This wasn't just about going to college; my manhood was on the line.

When spring break came that year, my parents had already moved to North Mississippi. I expected my parents to drive to Mount Olive to pick me up for my week-long break. In my weekly phone call home, my father told me "We're not coming to Mount Olive to get you. I want you to take the bus." Even though I was sixteen years old, incredibly unsophisticated, and from a one-traffic-light town in Mississippi, I still thought taking the bus fell several notches below my dignity. Besides, my father had made me ride the bus once before from Biloxi to Mount Olive, an experience I counted as one of the lowest points of my life. Wasn't that enough? On that trip he insisted that I have the driver drop me at the intersection of Highway 49 and Highway 35, the road that led to our house, rather than at the depot in town. Of course, I did as I was told and walked off the bus onto the hot Mississippi blacktop, with my Boy Scout backpack slung across my shoulder. I trudged home feeling like an abandoned hobo, cursing his name with every step.

"Riding the bus toughens you up and you always meet interesting people," he told me in a long tirade. Clearly he thought I had been pampered and needed to spend more time around people who were not as privileged as I was. Deep down, I knew my father was right. Riding the bus did make me see how easy my life was. The drunken factory worker I met on the bus from Biloxi had never even thought of going to college, much less Ole Miss or Tulane. What did I really have to complain about? Then my father added, "and the bus goes through Oxford, so maybe you could stop and take a look at Ole Miss." So on a chilly Friday morning in March of 1974, against my will, I boarded the Trailways bus to Jackson at Tolleson's Grocery Store on Main Street, hoping that on this bus trip I would maintain my dignity. At least this time my father promised to meet me at the depot.

The passengers I encountered when I boarded the bus in Mount Olive seemed perfectly normal. But I imagined that drunks and drifters just like the ones who had accompanied me on my trip from Biloxi would be boarding the bus in Jackson. To my surprise, I was wrong. Like the other public schools, the School for the Deaf in Mississippi was also on spring break. The bus quickly filled with quiet, neat, deaf students on their way home to all of those little towns the bus passed through along the way: Duck Hill, Durant, Vaiden, Grenada, Batesville. So, I read *The Great Gatsby* in paperback surrounded by the quiet of a busload of deaf teenagers as we drove through the edge of the

Delta, eagerly awaiting the stop in Oxford my father had arranged for me.

At the time of that bus ride I had been accepted at Ole Miss even though I had never visited the campus. All my life, Oxford was a place to be avoided, since my mother had essentially refused to set foot on soil that even bordered Ole Miss. My first look at the University of Mississippi, the place where I would spend my last four years in Mississippi, came from the rain-streaked window of a Trailways bus that drove past the edge of campus, providing only a fleeting glimpse of a few buildings. The bus was behind schedule for its final destination, Tupelo, so I didn't have time to walk the campus as I had planned. I did stroll through Courthouse Square, and it looked just as I had imagined the town of Jefferson described in William Faulkner's novels, only grander. At that moment I couldn't wait to begin at Ole Miss. I was smitten by the town of Oxford.

Right off the square I spotted a restaurant called the Gumbo Company that had a New Orleans–style balcony and served Creole food. Since I wasn't going to get to New Orleans to go to Tulane, at least a little taste of New Orleans resides in Oxford, I thought, and that was just going to have to do.

Ole Miss. Those two words evoke so many images of Mississippi and the South for me. When I think of Ole Miss, a vivid picture of its calm, pastoral campus, with majestic oak and maple trees, Greek Revival and Gothic buildings, such as the main administration building, the Lyceum, and favorite gathering spot called "the Grove," a lush, neatly manicured green on the edge of campus, instantly comes to mind. After years of conflicted feelings, the independence of my decision to attend Ole Miss has come to overshadow any bitterness about my rocky four years there. Ole Miss was not my first choice, but it was my choice. That feeling hit me as I retraced my bus ride from Jackson to Oxford in a rented car, with B.B. King playing in the background, telling me that you can always keep moving if you don't look down. By the time I drove through the streets of Oxford that day, I looked at them just as I did when I first stepped off that Trailways bus. The sheer beauty of the place overwhelmed any anger. I had stopped looking down. At last, Ole Miss belonged to me.

It is hard, though, not to look down on Ole Miss. For many, it will be forever linked with the dark events of September 30, 1962, when the air was filled with the smell of tear gas and the lush grounds of the Grove were littered with tear-gas canisters. As James Meredith waited to register as Ole Miss's first black student, that was the scene playing around him. Since that day, that same scene of mayhem has come to represent Ole Miss in the nation's memory.

On the evening before Meredith registered, students gathered with townspeople from nearby Oxford, as well as throngs of other segregationists from across the South who came to fight against the integration of Ole Miss, creating a melee that lasted well into the next morning. When it was over two people were dead, 166 Federal marshals and 40 soldiers were injured, and 30,000 combat troops had been called in by President Kennedy to quell the violence. The places I cherish and think of as peaceful, the Grove and the Lyceum, were ravaged like a battlefield. Some even refer to September 30 and October 1, 1962, as "the Battle of Oxford," since the State of Mississippi slid into a revolt against the Federal Government for the first time since the Civil War.

If you look closely at the Lyceum today, you can still see the bullet holes. They are tiny, almost minute, dwarfed by the columns that stand in front of them. But those holes in the walls of the Lyceum building, the physical symbol of this university and its ties to the Old South, serve as a memorial to the battle of Oxford, one of a series of battles that eventually toppled the Jim Crow traditions of the old South. Many would like to forget that the artfully patched bullet holes exist, for they do often over-shadow many years of progress in Mississippi and at Ole Miss. I have always felt a kinship with them, from my first day at Ole Miss, and always knew that those bullet holes paved the way for me to be accepted there.

I haven't felt the same kinship with the man who made it possible for me to attend Ole Miss, however. James Meredith is an enigmatic rather than approachable figure, a hero more mysterious than engaging. According to Constance Baker Motley, his attorney from the NAACP Defense Fund, "Meredith had to have a messiah complex to do what he did." Another NAACP attorney, Jack Greenberg, felt that "Meredith was a man with a mission. He acted like he was an agent of God." Perhaps that is why I connected with the bullet-battered walls of the Lyceum rather than with the man who sparked the battle that put them there. I ended up at Ole Miss by chance, like the bullet holes, rather than by an act of messianic zeal.

I did identify with James Meredith in his great love of Mississippi. It was that love and his desire to carve out a place there for his family that motivated Meredith to attend Ole Miss. He wasn't motivated purely by fulfilling what seemed like an impossible mission. "Without fail, regardless of the number of times I enter Mississippi, it creates within me feelings that are felt at no other time," Meredith wrote in his book *Three Years in Mississippi*, echoing how I feel each time I arrive in the Magnolia State. "I can love Mississippi because of the beauty of the countryside and the old traditions of family affection, and for such small things as flowers bursting in spring and the way you can see for miles from a ridge in winter. Why should a Negro be forced to leave such things? Because of fear? Not anymore."

And Meredith did show that he was fearless. I always knew that the persistence and tenacity Meredith displayed during the integration of Ole Miss were characteristics to be emulated. I aspired to have that kind of courage. So on my first day on campus in the fall of 1974, I walked to the Lyceum as one might visit a shrine. I wanted to see the bullet holes, to touch them, perhaps to gain some of Meredith's mettle and drive. Over the next four years, they would become a touchstone for me and I would cast respectful glances at them as I cut through the Lyceum on my way to class.

What Meredith endured made my time at Ole Miss easier; there is no denying that. No, it wasn't easy being a black student at Ole Miss in the early 1970s, for the wounds from the integration of Ole Miss were still open and festering. I like to think that my time at the University of Mississippi contributed to healing those wounds. I know that I am a better person because of my time at Ole Miss.

My freshman year began twelve years after Meredith came to Ole Miss and flanked by Federal marshals walked up the bloodstained steps of the Lyceum to register for classes. In spite of the number of years in between, Meredith remained a force to be reckoned with there. Meredith still rankled the Ole Miss administration and the white establishment. An interview with him on a nationally televised football game between Ole Miss and the University of Alabama in the fall of 1974 caused a firestorm of negative letters by white students and alumni to the school paper, the *Daily Mississippian*. Almost any mention of Meredith or the events of September 30, 1962, set off a defensive posture, be it from the administration of the university, current students, or alumni.

The Sovereignty Commission stood at the pinnacle of its power during Meredith's time at Ole Miss, watching his every move and working closely with Governor Barnett to block his admission. In the days leading up to Meredith's arrival at Ole Miss, the Sovereignty Commission operated in a crisis mode. Six hundred postcards addressed to President Kennedy were printed, denouncing the government's "unnatural warfare" against Mississippi. A small fleet of private planes flew out of Jackson to deliver the postcards for distribution to weekend football crowds across the South.

After Meredith was admitted, the Sovereignty Commission continued monitoring his movements. The Commission kept tabs on white students and faculty who shared meals with him and planted a student informant in the class of Russell Barrett, a political science professor who supported Meredith's admission. The Commission's classroom spy is mentioned in the manuscript of Barrett's book, *Integration at Ole Miss*. Barrett's editor was incredulous about the spying and wrote a pointed query in the margin asking if he was sure about his claim. In the finished book, the editor did not let the paragraph stand as it was originally written, making the spying claim less pointed and direct. Now, with the opening of the Sovereignty Commission files, Russell Barrett's claim can be verified. And I don't think he would be surprised by the lack of accuracy in the spies' reports.

Lone students were not the only Sovereignty Commission spies at Ole Miss in 1962. Segregationist student groups, such as the "Rebel Underground" and another calling itself the "Knights of the Forest, University of Mississippi" also served as part of the information-gathering network. The Knights of the Forest supplied then Sovereignty Commission public relations director Erle Johnston with its own list of "integrationists" at Ole Miss, independent of the Rebel Underground. The Rebel Underground, an anonymous broadside dedicated to the preservation of "your racial heritage," was monitored by the Sovereignty Commission, largely as a source of information for its files. Though none of the inflammatory claims made by the Rebel Underground against Ole Miss professors, including Russell Barrett and history professor James Silver, were entirely true, the Sovereignty Commission collected them for their files as evidence nevertheless.

Just a few months before Meredith's graduation in 1963, the Sovereignty Commission presented a resolution to the Chancellor of the University of Mississippi requesting an investigation to determine if Meredith had violated the chancellor's directive that students not give statements to the news media "that would be harmful to the University of Mississippi." Of course this was just a ploy to prevent Meredith from receiving an Ole Miss diploma. Though the effort failed and Meredith graduated, a great deal of the Sovereignty Commission's time and resources was spent on trying to find a way to get James Meredith kicked out of Ole Miss.

By 1970, with Mississippi schools and public facilities completely integrated, the Sovereignty Commission lacked both political power and financial resources. Maintaining segregation was a lost cause, and the Commission's budget and influence had dwindled to the point that it was virtually powerless. All that remained was a bureaucracy that struggled to justify its existence from year to year. Still, it tried to wield its influence wherever and whenever it could and with whatever resources it could muster. One of the places its work continued was at Ole Miss.

Up until 1973, just months before it closed its doors, the Sovereignty Commission and its investigators were monitoring activities on the Ole Miss campus. The university police department served as its primary information source; the chief of police routinely turned over information to the Sovereignty Commission on police reports as varied as arrests for marijuana possession to the dates and times of the meetings of "The Coalition for Progress," a group that was pushing for opposite-sex visitation in dormitories. A series of reports and investigations marked "This is a list of black students; file in the University of Mississippi file" was kept until 1970, as were copies of the newsletters of the university's Black Student Union. Had I come to Ole Miss a mere four years earlier, it is possible that I would have joined my parents in the Sovereignty Commission files.

After 1970, the Sovereignty Commission continued its investigations purely to provide information to state legislators who held Ole Miss's purse strings, many of whom were Ole Miss graduates. Although these legislators could not stop integration at Ole Miss, they fought to keep what they saw as its remaining traditions intact. Never known to be keen investigators, the Sovereignty Commission had no idea that tensions were mounting among black students at Ole Miss.

A protest by black students in February 1970, demanding that the university's chancellor respond to a list of concerns about campus life for black students, brought Sovereignty Commission investigators to campus to monitor the situation. This investigation led to a series of reports in the files that reveal the complete cooperation of the university police department in providing names and personal information on the students involved. By the time the protest episode was over, eight black students had been expelled from Ole Miss and the remaining forty-five protesters were given ten years probation. "This should asure (*sic*) that they won't be involved in any more disturbance," wrote Sovereignty Commission investigator Fulton Tutor in March 1970.

All of this may seem trivial today, but Ole Miss and Mississippi in the early 1970s remained virtually paralyzed by a racially charged past. The student body at Ole Miss was still overwhelmingly white, with a mere smattering of blacks. Out of my freshman class of over 800, there were only about 50 black students. The faculty in 1974 included only two black members, both in the school of social work and neither of them full professors. Campus social life was still largely segregated, with student government dominated by white fraternities and sororities. Black students were relegated to the Black Student Union and their own Greek-letter organizations and held no campus-wide student government offices. At the time, an attitude still existed among whites in the state that blacks could attend Ole Miss, but that was all they could do. The culture, heritage, and traditions of the school stood as barriers, since those were the domain of the dominant white culture and would remain. Integration may have broken a legal barrier for blacks to attend Ole Miss, but the barriers of a white culture and its traditions were stronger, almost impenetrable.

Mount Olive, in some ways, conditioned me for my time at Ole Miss. I had faced isolation when I landed in an all-white classroom in eighth grade and as a result learned self-reliance and gained the ability to ignore any insults hurled my way. If I had to, I could call on those skills again at Ole Miss. But Ole Miss represented not just a racial divide but a cultural one as well: The Confederate era still held sway there and was brandished in your face at every turn. That was something I had never faced before, except for the few weeks when we studied the "War for Southern Independence" at Mount Olive. This was different, since this cultural chasm seemed unbridgeable.

On the one hand, Ole Miss was a welcoming and encouraging place, even giving some degree of personal attention to the black students in the freshman class to encourage us to stay the whole four years. On the other hand, however, Ole Miss existed as a world unto itself, like one big memorial to the lost cause of the Confederacy. Ole Miss gave the outward impression that it was digging around the edges of Jim Crow and deeper into the culture of the Old South. Though that was not an entirely accurate impression, student comments sometimes branded Ole Miss with the negative image it sought to avoid. In 1979, the year after my graduation, when the topic of removing the Rebel flag as a symbol of Ole Miss was discussed, a student complained that if some people had their way, Ole Miss would be named the "University of Medgar Evers."

Rebel flags carried by young men in Confederate dress at sporting events at Ole Miss conveyed the message that blacks would always be excluded from the culture at Ole Miss. How could the descendants of slaves want to be a part of the traditions that represented an era when their great-grandparents were in bondage?

Even the name Ole Miss has its roots in that era of bondage. "Ole Miss" comes from a shortened version of "Old Missy," the name slaves would have called the wife of the plantation owner. The daughter of the plantation owner was the "young miss," the wife the "ole miss." Needless to say, this reference to plantation aristocracy, when blacks were slaves and whites were masters, made many black students uncomfortable. But the Civil War, as much as the plantation culture, stood as the basis of Ole

Miss's identity. During the war, the entire student body and faculty left Ole Miss and enlisted for duty, and most banded together as the University Greys and served the Confederacy. Ole Miss was closed for most of the war, and those students who served the Confederacy did not return when it reopened in 1865. It is in honor of the University Greys that Ole Miss's mascot is called "Colonel Rebel," that the Confederate flag was at one time displayed at all sporting events, and that the band played "Dixie" as the Ole Miss football team came onto the field. Ole Miss may have had to admit black students, but it wasn't going to disassociate itself from symbols like the Confederate flag, symbols that most blacks found offensive and that contributed to a hostile, racially polarizing environment.

All of this was compounded by the belief among many black Mississippians that blacks who attended Ole Miss were nothing more than sellouts and Uncle Toms. How could any self-respecting black person cheer on a team called the Rebels? References to Ole Miss were often made with a sneer and tone of condescension that said "real black people don't go to Ole Miss." Among my classmates, I heard stories of their being booed in church when the preacher announced they were going to Ole Miss. Special prayers were sometimes requested for young members of black churches before they went to Ole Miss, with the women in the "amen corner" saying, "Y'all better pray for these children hard, 'cause they sure are going to need it."

We did need those prayers. We needed them not because of any threats of violence against us or truly overt racism. We needed them because the social barriers were like nothing most of us had ever experienced. The first social barrier came about in dormitory living, for most black students had come from towns like mine, where the racial lines were firmly drawn and were crossed knowing that violence was a consequence. For many of the white students, they had never gone to school with a black person, much less lived next door to one.

When James Meredith arrived at Ole Miss in 1962, he was in a dormitory with Federal Marshalls. In June 1963, he was given a roommate, Cleve McDowell, who, after a brief court battle, became the second black student at Ole Miss. Meredith and McDowell were assigned to a dormitory by themselves, and no other students were assigned dorms at their end of the Ole Miss campus. McDowell's first semester at Ole Miss was Meredith's last.

Unlike James Meredith, I was assigned a white roommate.

By 1974, Ole Miss did not make dormitory roommate assignments based on race. When I moved into my dorm room at Twin Towers, my roommate, Mark Crain, had already settled in and decorated the room in typical Ole Miss fashion: a Confederate flag was placed right above his bed. After I opened the door with an armload of clothes, we shook hands and I introduced him to my father, who had come to help me move in. Both my father and I ignored the flag, but I was having a difficult time not noticing it. It was so big it almost filled the entire wall. "Just don't pay any attention to that Rebel flag," my father said to me soothingly after Mark left for the afternoon. My father sensed that its prominence made me uncomfortable. "If you're going to survive here, you're just going to have to get used to seeing them everywhere," he added. Although I knew he was right, being in the same room with the flag was not the same as seeing it off in the distance on a football field. I continued to unpack and then we went out to lunch before my father left to go home.

When I came back, the flag had been taken down.

"I didn't want to offend you with the flag," Mark told me later that evening, when he came back from a fraternity rush party. As we talked about Ole Miss and the Confederate flag, it became clear that he was just as conflicted about the flag as I was. Mark recognized that the flag was more than just a symbol of Ole Miss, that it was offensive to black people because of its use by racist groups. He didn't want me to think of him as a racist.

Most black students weren't as lucky as I was with their roommate assignment. I heard over and over of the same chain of events: black roommate walks up to the door, white roommate looks up in stunned silence, and moves out. Sometimes an ugly confrontation erupted, but often the white roommate just moved out in stoney silence. Tales of the "startled white roommate" abounded among black students at Ole Miss, many of the stories ending with black roommates finding themselves together because another white student with a black roommate put them together. Now that housing was re-segregated by the students, the next hurdle to get over was Ole Miss's social system.

Ole Miss was also heavily divided along class lines, with the fraternity and sorority system dominating the social and political scene of the campus. Attending Ole Miss was viewed as a birthright for that segment of the student population. Conversely, many of the black students were the first in their families to go to college. Though many of my fellow black freshmen had confronted racism in Mississippi's newly integrated high schools, class combined with the ingrained Confederate-era traditions of Ole Miss complicated the already tense dynamic of integration.

Rather than meeting the situation head on, many black students succumbed to Ole Miss's class system and isolated themselves as a means of coping with what felt like an unwelcoming environment. Others eventually transferred to predominantly black colleges in the state. Most of us who stayed were committed to creating some kind of change and knew that change would not come if we retreated into our own worlds. Student government and politics seemed to be the great equalizers at Ole Miss, so I chose these routes to make a difference. If white students who were not Ole Miss legacies were elected to office, I decided I could do the same.

In the fall of 1975, armed with campaign material I had developed, I ran for campus senate from my dormitory. Like a good politician, I visited every room in the eleven floors of my dormitory, Twin Towers. If no one was in the room, I left a card with a personal note inscribed on the back asking for votes. On election day, I handed out my campaign cards to people as they got off the elevator and asked them to vote for me. No longer was I the quiet, retiring boy from a small town in Mississippi. I was a shameless, glad-handing politician. And I loved it. The campaign strategy worked and I was elected, along with two other black students. We became the first black students elected to the campus senate.

My involvement in campus politics did not give me much hope for substantial change at Ole Miss, but it did give me more personal confidence. During my freshman year, I had spent most of my time involved with my studies and very little time on social activities. Now that I was a campus politician, I became more outgoing socially, and many of the people I made social ties with were white. Although I knew that I was crossing an invisible social line, I crossed it anyway. If I was cocky enough to get myself elected to the campus senate, I wasn't going to let anyone dictate who my friends could be.

When I overheard black students criticizing me for going to "Dixie Week" dances, organizing an Earth Day celebration in the Grove, or other social activities deemed to be for whites only, I felt hurt and betrayed. It also hurt when white students looked at me as if I didn't belong at those activities, or as if it was inappropriate for me to take a leadership role directing a group of white volunteers. Often I felt confused and alone—confused because I didn't understand what I was doing wrong and alone because no one else seemed to think I was doing right.

By this point in my career at Ole Miss, I had evolved from a pre-med major to a psychology and English literature major. Victorian literature had become my great love, but Faulkner still held me rapt in his spell. In fact, a quote from his Nobel

Prize acceptance speech, inscribed on the wall of the Ole Miss Library, inspired me to get through those years. It said, "I decline to accept the end of man. I believe that man will not merely endure, he will prevail." I pondered that quote a great deal during my time there and before long adapted Faulkner's words for my situation: "I decline to accept the Old South; I choose to prevail over it rather than endure it." The spirit of defiance I found in those words, coupled with my willful independence, helped me persevere.

After my sophomore year, I chose not to run for the campus senate again. Though still involved in a number of campus organizations, I chose to stay on the periphery rather than at the center. Besides, I needed to figure out what to do with my life once I graduated. I had left high school determined to leave Mississippi, and I didn't want to get stuck in Mississippi after graduating from Ole Miss. Again, the brochures began to arrive in the mail from schools far away from Mississippi, but this time from outside the South.

A few months before graduation, my chance to leave Mississippi finally came. A letter arrived from the University of Michigan accepting me into a graduate program in English language and literature. My professors in the English department were thrilled. One even suggested that I go on to a doctorate and come back to teach at Ole Miss. For a fleeting moment, the idea appealed to me, perhaps because I thought I would be able to help other black students like me who came seeking not just a degree, but knowledge, knowledge of themselves and the world outside of Mississippi. But deep in my heart I knew I was no longer content to stay in Mississippi. I felt confined from the world I knew lay outside of its borders, the world I had been thirsting for since I was sixteen years old. Though I had no idea of what I wanted to do with my life, I knew one thing: I could not figure out the rest of my life if I stayed in Mississippi.

My father never lived to see me graduate from Ole Miss. The man who sent me to Oxford on a bus ride hoping I would encounter a few hard knocks died my sophomore year, leaving me to figure out the rest of my life largely on my own. I didn't leave Ole Miss for medical school, the path he felt I should follow, the one he viewed as a clear route to success. My path was much more uncertain, as evidenced by my wandering around England and Ireland the summer after graduation, doing everything from herding cattle in County Leitrim to washing pint glasses in a London pub. By the time I arrived in Ann Arbor in the fall, my career plans were still up in the air, but one thing was certain: I had left Mississippi forever. Even after a long, cold Michigan winter, I was certain deep inside that there was nothing that would ever draw me back there.

Part THREE

Searching for the Truth

❖　　❖　　❖

The excursion is the same when you go looking for
your sorrow as when you go looking for your joy.
— Eudora Welty, "The Wide Net"

EIGHT

Facing the Firebrand

After months of poring over Sovereignty Commission memos, letters, and correspondence and revisiting Mississippi's tortured past, I began to wonder how much of Mississippi's past remained in the present. In Mississippi, as William Faulkner noted, the past is never dead; it's not even past. During my adolescence and young adulthood, living with remnants of Mississippi's lingering past became so unbearable that I had to leave; in middle age, the same forces from the past had drawn me back. Rather than running away again, I had to understand this past that never dies and somehow reconcile it with the present. At this stage in my journey back to Mississippi, I believed the way to do that was to get to the truth behind sketchy information I had found in the Sovereignty Commission files.

To begin this reconciliation, I traveled around more on my trips to Mississippi and spent less time in the archives steeping myself in the past. What I began to look for were the lingering cultural influences of the Sovereignty Commission. From all the documents I read, the Commission's strongest impact had been to create a culture that tolerated violence and mistreatment of black citizens. In the quarter of a century since it closed its doors, how much of the culture of the Sovereignty Commission remained?

One afternoon in Jackson I lingered after lunch rather than rushing back to the archives and just observed the smattering of people in and around downtown. As I began to watch ordinary people in ordinary places around Mississippi, I recognized little of the past in what I encountered: a friendly lunch conversation among an integrated group of businessmen in Jackson about their after-work basketball game; an interracial couple with their children in tow shopping at a Wal-Mart in Magee; African-American legislators working the corridors of the state capitol. Such scenes were nonexistent during my childhood, and rare during my time at Ole Miss.

Soon I felt a resurgence of pride in being from Mississippi, something I hadn't felt in a long time, but just as I began to feel reconnected, a sign of the old Mississippi rose up: In a statewide referendum in the spring of 2001, Mississippi voted to keep the racially charged Confederate flag as part of its state flag. Suddenly, I felt the shadow of the Sovereignty Commission casting itself on the present. My pride sank.

Many white Mississippians at the dawn of the twenty-first century showed as much resistance to removing the Confederate battle flag as a symbol as they did to racial integration in the 1960s. Even the language Confederate flag proponents used to justify their resistance bore a striking resemblance to the defense of segregation under the guise of states' rights. Segregationist state legislators used the word *encroachment* in the charter of the Sovereignty Commission to appeal to Mississippians' desire to keep their society closed and to protect the racial status quo; Confederate flag proponents used words such as *heritage* and *tradition* to appeal to those who wanted to cling to the one remaining symbol of Mississippi left from the era of segregation. As I followed the debate over the state flag, I couldn't help but recognize that elements of the pre–Civil Rights movement era were alive and well in Mississippi, yet artfully hidden. Although Mississippi had broken free of the racial conformity that the Sovereignty Commission worked so diligently to maintain, there was still darkness amidst the light.

After emerging from Mississippi's past in the Sovereignty Commission files and delving into the new Mississippi, I began to wonder: Did the people who fought change in Mississippi still believe that their fight to keep the old way of life was right? From what I could see, remnants of that culture remained in the minds of some, but I had also observed how Mississippi had changed. Had these people changed as well? It was hard to tell, especially after I read a poll in March 2001 on the flag referendum in the *Clarion-Ledger* in which some white Mississippians believed "too many concessions" had already been made to black people. In another article, I encountered this quote for keeping the Confederate battleflag in the state flag: "I don't believe in turning over to what the colored people want. We've got our rights, too."

During its reign, the Sovereignty Commission cast a shadow over the lives of so many people. Seeing the old Mississippi rise up in the debate over the state flag made it clear to me that the shadow is present even today. In the wake of these events, I knew what I had to do. Somehow I had to find the people who had aligned themselves with the Sovereignty Commission and believed in what it purported to do.

After digging around in the Mississippi Department of Archives and History, I discovered that there were few people still alive who were part of the Commission's inner circle. The governors of Mississippi at the height of the Sovereignty Commission's power were dead; others, such as the one-time public relations director and head of the Sovereignty Commission itself, Erle Johnston, had long been dead. Two years before his death in 1995, Johnston told historian Yasuhiro Katagiri as part of a Civil Rights-era oral history project, "I could not have realized that the civil rights struggle in Mississippi was fought only for the state's black folks, but for us whites . . . It was for the redemption of our white souls." Based on what I found in this interview, Johnston gave the outward impression of having had a change of heart. That said, I also knew from the files that he was a public-relations mastermind, a major force in maintaining the culture of the closed society in Mississippi. Did his oral history reflect a real change, or just a calculated strategy to polish his image for the history books? I'll never know that answer. Once again, I realized that if I wanted to experience the impact Mississippi's change had on those who had fought to maintain a segregated society, I would have to discover it through documents.

My quest began in the family papers of former Mississippi governor Paul B. Johnson, which contained Sovereignty Commission reports he received during his term. As I paged through the chronology of Johnson's time as governor from 1964 to 1968, I saw reports from the Sovereignty Commission that crossed his desk scattered among legislative and political issues, including details of the Commission's investigation of the Civil Rights movement during the summer of 1964. Throughout the summer there were reports from the Commission about the disappearance of the three civil rights workers in Philadelphia, Mississippi: Andrew Goodman, James Chaney, and Michael Schwerner. By the fall, the Commission went county by county to investigate the aftermath of Freedom Summer, including a visit to the sheriff of Covington County to see if there were any voter registration schools in the county and any "trouble" from the NAACP. For the first time, I realized how the documents I had viewed by subject and place on a computer screen were actually used by a sitting governor. Now I understood how a personal letter to the governor could launch a Sovereignty Commission investigation of an organization, as it did with the Extension Service in the case of my father. I also saw documents I had not seen in the main archives of the Sovereignty Commission in Jackson, a sign that some key incriminating pieces of information had probably been destroyed.

Though there was a flurry of investigations during the summer of 1964 and into the fall, the Sovereignty Commission moved into a period of relative dormancy in its aftermath. The events of that summer and their tie to Sovereignty Commission investigations troubled Governor Johnson, leading him by 1965 to proclaim before the U.S. Commission on Civil Rights that Mississippians would accept the Civil Rights Act of 1964 "in a calm, intelligent manner, regardless of personal conviction." From what I could see in his papers, as early as the fall of 1964, Governor Johnson had begun to rethink the role of the Sovereignty Commission. By no means had the murders of Goodman, Chaney, and Schwerner changed the man who "stood tall" against admitting James Meredith to Ole Miss into a racial moderate. But they had forced him to approach his stand on segregation with greater caution.

As I paged through the files that contained material on the aftermath of the murder of the three Civil Rights workers, another item stood out. It was a one-sentence letter from January 1965, six months after the murders, from state representative and Sovereignty Commission member Horace Harned that read, "Is Mississippi going to have a Sovereignty Commission?" Governor Johnson replied, "I have felt the need to delay the matter for this period of time." Beginning with a series of recommendations from the director of the Sovereignty Commission Erle Johnston, the governor had been considering whether the Commission's investigations were making matters better or worse in Mississippi. Horace Harned was persistent in his insistence that Mississippi have a Sovereignty Commission, and put forth a resolution demanding the activation of the watchdog group.

Paul Johnson died in 1985, and the opening of his papers in 1989 effectively unleashed a number of Sovereignty Commission documents in his personal papers that were to be closed until 2023. Once the Sovereignty Commission documents in the Johnson papers were discovered, a court battle ensued regarding access to the documents, leading to the opening of the Sovereignty Commission files in 1998, twenty-five years before their scheduled opening. The only person left to explain this exchange with Governor Johnson was Horace Harned. In examining the papers of a dead man, I was finally led to someone I thought could explain some of what I found in the files.

Now in his eighties, Horace Harned is a retired state senator who served on the Sovereignty Commission from 1964 to 1968. Harned has a reputation as an unreconstructed racial firebrand. Initially I was reluctant to contact him, particularly after reading an oral history in the McCain Library at the University of Southern Mississippi in which he proudly proclaimed his involvement in forming a White Citizens' Council in his community. He even said that "the vast majority of our people, both black and white, were against forced integration." But after listening to an interview he gave to National Public Radio in the spring of 2001, I became intrigued by his unapologetic view of Mississippi's past. He spoke in that interview of his fear of a communist takeover in Mississippi and referred to the days of the Civil Rights movement as a time of war in Mississippi. Though I had read similar views in the Sovereignty Commission files, I had never heard those views uttered from the lips of someone who believed them and voiced them with such conviction. As a result, I decided to write him a letter:

Dear Mr. Harned:

In your recent National Public Radio interview, you stated that you do not often get a chance to explain your side of the Civil Rights story: "There are very few that are much interested in the story to pursue it and concentrate on it. If they are, I'll be glad to sit down and try to explain. I've got nothing to hide." Well, I am interested and would like to sit down and talk with you, even though my perspective may be different from yours. In spite of our differences, I am willing to listen.

A few weeks later a response arrived:

Dear Mr. Eubanks:

You put me on notice that you may not agree with me on all my positions. Take heart, no one does; not even my wife. We are each the sum total of all our experiences and our faith.

Enclosed with his response was a copy of a letter he had written to the editor of the Columbus, Mississippi, *Commercial Dispatch* in favor of keeping the Confederate battleflag as part of the state flag of Mississippi. In reference to the possibility of changing the state flag, Harned had written, "We are in spiritual warfare here."

The culture of the Sovereignty Commission lives on, I thought.

The past and the present collided in Horace Harned's letter. In the 1950s and 1960s the fight to maintain segregation was often characterized as an act of spiritual warfare. Clearly, here was a man who was still fighting on the battle lines drawn out by the Sovereignty Commission. He still held firm in the position he had in the 1960s. Horace Harned did not believe in letting the past die.

After a few telephone conversations, we planned to meet on my next trip to Mississippi. Two months after our initial correspondence, I awaited his arrival nervously in the lobby of a Ramada Inn in Starkville. Upon our meeting, his gracious manner immediately put me at ease.

He is a courtly, gray-haired Southern gentleman with a broad, toothy grin who bears little outward resemblance to the "firebrand segregationist" he says he once was. He grasped my hand firmly with both of his, smiled broadly, and said "Welcome back to Mississippi." I thought, how could anyone this gentle be an advocate for something so terrible as the Sovereignty Commission? His gesture wrenched the tension and nervousness out of my body, and soon we were sipping tea in a Chinese restaurant and bantering back and forth like old friends. Not until we began to talk about the Sovereignty Commission did the firebrand behind the grandfatherly façade start to come out.

After establishing the facts and the time he served on the Sovereignty Commission, Mr. Harned proclaimed that what he fought for was "to maintain our state's rights and our racial integrity. I don't think the government should be involved in social engineering." In his opinion, the most significant aspect of the Sovereignty Commission was that "it gave the people assurance that their leaders were trying to protect their interests."

And what were those interests? Again, he said states' rights and racial integrity. Though he would never define states' rights or racial integrity, he spoke of them as if I knew exactly what each meant. And I did; through the files, I had become familiar with the code. Horace Harned spoke the code fluently.

"I was the firebrand on the Sovereignty Commission," he said, in answer to my question of what prompted him to write the letter to Governor Paul B. Johnson that I had found in the Johnson papers. "I wanted to get something done. I had much more knowledge of the Civil Rights movement and the communist infiltration than anyone else." When I pressed him about the source of his information, he remarked matter of factly that his vast knowledge of the Civil Rights movement came from his membership in the John Birch Society and his involvement in the Citizens' Council. Though I chose not to challenge his sources, I was struck by the power that the propaganda of these two groups continued to hold on this man. Clearly, he was still under the spell of McCarthyism, Mississippi style.

Harned felt that the Sovereignty Commission had become inactive under Johnson, and more than anything he wanted to protect Mississippi from "the big threat coming to upset our culture down here." The only way he saw to do that was by having an active Sovereignty Commission. I reminded him that based on my examination of the Johnson papers and given the amount of material in them from 1964 until 1968, the Sovereignty Commission had been very much alive and active. Governor Johnson merely held the card of the Sovereignty Commission close to his chest, keeping the Commission under his control to prevent any more brutal murders from happening in Mississippi over Civil Rights. The same man who campaigned throughout Mississippi in telling a joke about what NAACP stands for (niggers, alligators, apes, 'coons, possums) turned out to be a voice of moderation.

Harned quickly noted that Governor Johnson, by his almost solitary oversight of the Sovereignty Commission, had left nothing for people like him to do. And more than anything, he wanted to do something about what he saw as a communist invasion of Mississippi because of the Civil Rights movement.

I soon realized that Horace Harned justified his position on race by clinging to a view of standing up to communism, a stance that could not be argued with in America during the Cold War. I told him that I had come to listen to his side of the Civil Rights story, and though I listened politely to his list of communist ties to every Civil Rights group, including the National Council of Churches, I decided to change the subject. I wanted to hear what his vision was of the Sovereignty Commission. Did it want to target black professionals like my parents? I told him that my parents were NAACP members and were involved in voter registration but that that involvement had not landed them in the files.

"Well, that puts up a red flag right there," Harned said in response to learning of my parents' NAACP membership. "You know the NAACP was organized by the communists. It was a communist organization."

I was getting nowhere in the conversation and communism was coming up at every turn. To change his tape, I asked him what the Commission could do if information from the files was turned over to law enforcement in Mississippi. I demanded a straight answer. Since I had begun my work with the Sovereignty Commission files I had often wondered about what would have happened had my parents' NAACP involvement been revealed, placing them under closer surveillance. Would information have been turned over to their employers, or the county sheriff, as it had in the case of the three murdered Civil Rights workers? Did their Sovereignty Commission file place them in the same danger? Were my parents the kind of people a Sovereignty Commission investigator thought should be targeted? I had to know.

There was a pause in the conversation, as he pondered the question. "Those fellas," referring to Goodman, Chaney, and Schwerner, "came down here looking for trouble and they got it. Young folks, if they are looking for something they are going to find it. And there will be some rednecks out there that will accommodate them; I'll guarantee it. And there are still some of them there."

I was stunned. Though I had been direct with him, I still hadn't gotten a straight answer. In spite of feeling that the murder of the Civil Rights workers was "a big stain on the people of Mississippi," Horace Harned still believed that the Sovereignty Commission was necessary and served a useful function. "We were making the last stand to preserve the rights of the states to govern themselves," he said without a tone of remorse in his voice. That told me that anyone, even my parents, were possible targets.

Before we finished our lunch, I asked Mr. Harned if he thought the Sovereignty Commission files should have been opened. He gave me a stern and unequivocal "No." As I tried to probe more, he took control of the conversation, changed the topic to farming, and invited me out to see his farm and to continue our conversation there. I didn't argue; he had spoken fondly of his farm during the conversation, so I thought "why not?" The old Mississippi farm boy in me kind of wanted to see his place.

I followed his truck down a rolling country road to the farm he owns on his family's old plantation land. As we drove down his long gravel driveway, he pulled his truck up on the grass. I proceeded to park my car at the back of the house, where I saw another car parked. When I got out of the car, he yelled out to me and motioned with his hands to come over to him.

"Mr. Eubanks, I wanted you to park up here. I wanted to make sure you went through the front door." The unreconstructed racial firebrand did not want a black man entering his house through the back door. I explained that I could never park a car on someone else's grass, since my father felt that driving on someone's yard was incredibly rude and displayed a lack of respect for property. "I won't hold it against you if I go through the back," I told him. A visible grin spread across his face, he chuckled, and we went into his living room by way of the kitchen.

When we sat down, Mr. Harned told me that on the drive he had been doing some thinking about whether the Sovereignty Commission files should have been opened or not. "I may not be too consistent on whether the files should have been opened. I didn't think there would be anything in there that would harm anyone to any great degree. I didn't know what was in the files myself, and I didn't know that people would be so resentful of being in the files. But I can understand now why they would be, because they were under suspicion."

He then commented that my father's name in a Sovereignty Commission file came about as a result of an investigation of integrated meetings of county agents and extension home economists. "Any citizen could request an investigation of any person or any group," he added. "Why, I'm even in the files, too!" After our meeting, I looked at his file. There's nothing embarrassing there, only a request for an investigation of an effort to integrate his church in Starkville. The fact that any citizen could request a probe of anything they thought was suspicious or violated Mississippi's racial codes chilled me.

Even though I told Mr. Harned that I came to listen to his side, I still had to ask him a number of questions. Did he think paid informants were a good idea? He did, of course. And why did he change his mind on the ride out about the opening of the Sovereignty Commission files?

"Had the files not been opened, you would not be here today, would you? We wouldn't be able to talk like this, would we?" he said pointedly.

I agreed that we would not. Two men so different, with completely different points of view, would not be able to sit and have an open conversation in a society that Mr. Harned himself admits was closed to any opposing opinion. Yet here we were, a black man and a white man talking about race, politics, the errors of the past, and the promise of the present. By the time we finished talking, Horace Harned was almost crowing about the progress Mississippi had made, boasting about a report issued on the day of our interview that Mississippi had more black elected officials than any other state in the country. Yes, he clung to the vestiges of the past, but deep down I recognized that he knew the new Mississippi held a promise that he never thought existed. He just couldn't bring himself to admit it.

NINE

Down a Dark Trail

When I learned from the Sovereignty Commission files that a man who was a Ku Klux Klan member put my mother and every black teacher in Mount Olive in those same files, purely for the purpose of being watched, I could not imagine sitting down to talk with him. Spending time with a former member of the Sovereignty Commission was one thing; a Klansman was something altogether different. The idea of sitting down with someone who once masked himself in a white robe, went to cross burnings, and took part in an organization that terrorized black people repulsed me, to say the least. Would a white Mississippian even admit to a black man that he had been a member of the Klan? And, given his past affiliation, would he care that he helped out the Sovereignty Commission and risked endangering the life of my family?

From the time I arranged our meeting by telephone and up until the night before we met, I struggled with what I would say to Denson Lott, the man who put my mother in the Sovereignty Commission files. In our phone conversation, I was clear that I wanted to talk about the Sovereignty Commission, yet I purposely omitted that I wanted to talk about whether his Klan membership was a motivation for his cooperation with them. "I'm trying to piece together an understanding of what things were really like in Mount Olive and Covington County when I was growing up," I told him. He said he was willing to talk about his time as Superintendent of Education and tell me what he knew of the Sovereignty Commission. Of course, he told me how he remembered my family.

"Your mother had a wonderful smile, and there was no finer man than your daddy," he told me.

"Why, thank you, sir," I replied, remembering my manners. "It's very kind of you to say that." His comment put me at ease, but when I hung up the phone I resolved to maintain a sense of detachment, just as I had to do sometimes when reading much of the material I discovered in the Sovereignty Commission files. I felt a mixture of emotions as I looked at how the state of Mississippi spied on its own citizens. I wrestled with thoughts of how much of the old Mississippi's lived on and whether what I might unleash from the files would hurt me, and perhaps others. But if I could stand back and be objective, I thought, perhaps I would find answers to the questions that were causing my conflict.

My confusion and conflicted feelings about meeting Denson Lott stayed with me up until the night before our appointment. That evening, I discussed both with my high-school classmate, Jim Brewer. After not seeing each other for almost twenty-five years, Jim and I had become fast friends during my frequent trips to Mount Olive. As I sat in his living room, we talked about our memories of our first encounter in the eighth grade. That day was vividly imprinted on my memory. Jim had only the vaguest recollection of what I recalled as a turning point in my young life. That evening both of us came to a better understanding of how those early years of integration affected us, in different ways. We needed to understand those times better and as the evening wore on, we realized that understanding the past is what brought us together.

That night, Jim and his wife Kathy allowed me to free-associate over dinner about the man who in my mind was "Denson Lott, ex-Klansman." He wasn't a real person to me; I had fenced him into a stereotyped, race-baiting, cross-burning monster who helped the state spy on my mother and her colleagues. Like many of the people I read about in the Sovereignty Commission files, he didn't seem real.

"How are you going to get him to admit to you that he was a member of the Klan?" Jim asked me.

"I don't know," I said quietly. We talked over some of the questions I had for Lott; then I had a breakthrough.

"I'm going to ask him point blank if he was a member of the Klan," I said. "If he denies it, I'll just throw an article from the *Clarion-Ledger* I found in the Sovereignty Commission files that named him as a Klan member on the table. He can't deny that." In spite of my brief moment of braggadocio, I was prepared for a conversation that would end abruptly and without any satisfying resolution. I imagined an angry old man storming away from me, glaring and accusing me with, "How dare you bring this up? Who brought you up to do something like this?" And I had visions myself of walking away upset at not having elicited an answer and feeling guilty for making an old man wrestle with demons he had chosen to keep buried. After almost thirty years, Mount Olive's code of manners still had its grip.

"Is this the Denson Lott who lives out on the Sunset Road?" Kathy asked.

"Yes," I said. Kathy's family had lived outside of Mississippi most of her life while her father was in the Army. "You probably don't remember when he was Superintendent of Education."

"No, I don't," she said. "But, you know, I think he's some kin to me."

The three of us began to laugh, with Kathy laughing the loudest as she spotted the shock on my face. At that moment I think I lost whatever fear I had about the interview the next day. If Denson Lott was related to Kathy, albeit distantly, he must not be all bad. Finally, I felt comfortable and at home. I just had to keep those feelings throughout the next day.

"Be firm and factual," I repeated to myself as I drove down Highway 49 to Collins to meet Denson Lott for breakfast that sunny November morning. When I walked into Speck's Restaurant, Mr. Lott and I recognized each other right away. We shook hands and exchanged pleasantries, and he commented on how much I looked like my mother. After telling him a bit about myself, I decided to get down to business.

"Mr. Lott, as I told you, I wanted to talk with you about your time heading up the school system here in Covington County.

I'm not here to smear your name or make you feel bad; I just want to know the truth. When you were Superintendent of Education, you turned over a list of teachers' names to the Sovereignty Commission for possible investigation. Did you know at the time what those names could have been used for?"

"Well, Mr. Eubanks, I don't remember too much about doing that, but I'm sure that I did know what they could have been used for." We talked about how the workings of the Sovereignty Commission were largely kept closed from the public, so very little was explicit in conversations with their investigators. Then Mr. Lott looked directly at me, a sense of urgency on his face.

"What you need to know about me is that during that time, I was a member of the Ku Klux Klan down here. It's something I'm not proud of, but it's something I did do. And it affected a lot of things that I did."

My resolve crumbled as shock crossed my face. His admission changed what I thought was going to be a tense inquiry into a genuine conversation. I could see his shame and contrition. Suddenly the man who was a caricature in my mind became a real person.

"Well, Mr. Lott, I have to tell you that I knew about your Klan membership before I came here today." If he was going to be honest with me, I felt that I had to do the same. "I guess that now I don't have to ask you about it, but I do want to know more about why you were a member." Since the Klan is an organization that believes in white supremacy, I asked him if back during his time in the Klan he thought of himself as a white supremacist. He just laughed and shook his head.

"My membership in the Klan was for purely political reasons and I did it at my peril," he replied. I had heard of white men who, swept away in the fear and confusion of the Civil Rights era, joined organizations like the Klan and the Citizens' Council. When examined from the perspective of the present, it seems like a weak moral choice. However, the dominant code of behavior at work in the Mississippi of the 1960s was one that enforced segregation; anyone in a position of political power that chose a different point of view ran the risk of personal destruction. Membership in segregationist organizations was often one element of business and political survival, so strong was the sway those groups had on some towns. I never thought of Covington County as one of those places, but there was the possibility; the Klan was strong in neighboring Laurel and over in Sullivan's Hollow. I did know that from time to time the Klan had tried to wield its influence in Mount Olive and Collins, even burning a cross at the home of a white Baptist minister in Mount Olive as late as 1967. It made sense that the Klan would want the head of the school system among its members, since fighting school integration stood at the core of its local agenda.

Mr. Lott told me that he had rarely talked about his time in the Klan, even with his wife. His main reason for his involvement was simple, in his mind: "The Klan wanted to burn any school that might be integrated; as Superintendent of Education I wanted to keep schools from being burned. I tried to run the schools with an iron fist, and being a member of the Klan gave me the control I needed of the people who could have harmed the schools."

I tried to move the conversation away from the Klan to the Sovereignty Commission, which was primarily what I wanted to talk with him about. He remembered very little, mostly what I already knew. The Sovereignty Commission was keeping a record of the activities of all black teachers, which is why they came to him to get the list. He knew that if any of the teachers got involved with the NAACP or another group that the Sovereignty Commission would report it to him or to someone in law enforcement. As we talked about the Commission, our conversation moved back to his involvement with the Klan. His membership haunted him. I decided to listen rather than ask questions.

Mr. Lott confessed that he felt he was a captive of the circumstances in which he lived and that he walked a tense tightrope the whole time he was a Klan member. "There was violence going on all around us," he told me. "I wanted to keep it from coming here." The only way he saw to prevent violence was to align himself with the very people who would commit the acts.

"I took some dark trails back in those days," he said referring to his Klan membership. I began to wonder what he met on those dark trails and, moreover, who he met. Though I was sure it was a bleak, dark path, I wanted to know specifically what he had encountered. The most notorious Klansman around southern Mississippi was Samuel Bowers, who lived in nearby Laurel and was the Imperial Wizard of the White Knights of the Mississippi KKK. Bowers was suspected of being the mastermind behind at least nine murders, including the firebombing death of NAACP activist Vernon Dahmer in nearby Hattiesburg. Did he know Sam Bowers, a man who unleashed much of the terror and misery that surrounded Covington County? Was he trying to keep Sam Bowers out of Mount Olive and Collins?

I asked him.

At the mention of Samuel Bowers, his face took on a pained expression and became visibly tense. Even though Sam Bowers is now in jail for the murder of Vernon Dahmer, his name still elicits fear. And I saw that fear in Denson Lott's face. "My involvement with the Klan was not for the purpose of violence, but was purely political," he explained.

When he regained his composure, Mr. Lott began to talk again about why he was in the Klan. He did not want me to think of him as being cut from the same cloth as Sam Bowers. "My involvement with the Klan was quiet and with no fanfare. During those years, I owed my safety to God. If your heart is not right toward your fellow man, God will not listen." For years he knew that what he was doing was not right but kept his point of view to himself. Even though he dissolved his membership in the Klan in 1968, up until now he could never tell anyone how he really felt.

"My purpose was to have the best education we could have in Covington County without violence." He knew that integration was going to come to Covington County; still, he thought he had to manage the situation somehow.

"Mr. Eubanks, I don't think I'm a very intelligent man. That's why I did what I did." I chided him for saying something so demeaning, for knocking himself. But he wouldn't hear it. He felt strongly that his lack of intelligence was clear; the choice he made in allying himself with the Klan was not a sound decision. As he stared blankly across the table, with his face turned to the side, it was apparent that his membership in the Klan had wrecked him emotionally. His expression became contorted and his head dropped in shame when he related his involvement in the Klan.

There were still a few more things I wanted to know: Mr. Lott kept track of one side of the white community through his membership in the Klan, while working the other side through his political connections in the county and as a former state legislator. Did he have any black informants who fed him information?

The answer was "yes," and the name of my high-school friend's father and grandfather came up. "They told me everything," he said, including information from NAACP meetings and the fact that the local NAACP operated under a different name.

I was not surprised by this; it merely confirmed what I had heard as I talked with old family friends. That he corroborated it so matter of factly pained me nevertheless.

I had one more question: "Mr. Lott, do you have any regrets about the time you were Superintendent of Education?" I knew that he must, since walking what he described as the tightrope of his Klan membership must have caused tension and pain that might have been different had he chosen another way to accomplish his work. Though he had revealed a lot, I knew that much was still concealed to protect himself. I no longer felt judgmental about what he did, realizing that the decision he made had not been simple. I had only scratched the surface. But I knew from the Sovereignty Commission files that Mississippi whites felt so desperate and threatened by the changes they saw coming that they would do anything to maintain the status quo. Mr. Lott had gotten swept away in the desperation of the times. Did he regret it?

"I have nothing to regret," he told me. "All my decisions were designed to protect every person. My word was my bond, and a lie just wouldn't fit."

I thanked him for being so open with me. The conversation had not been easy for him. "It was very brave of you to tell me about your membership in the Klan without my having to pry it out of you," I told him quietly before we got up from the table. As we walked to the cash register I took the check from him.

"Oh, no, Mr. Eubanks. Let me get this for you," he said graciously.

I told him that I had asked him to breakfast. It was only fair that I pick up the check. He thanked me with an outpouring of gratitude mixed with sorrow in his voice, almost on the verge of tears. We shook hands, and he walked out of the restaurant.

I watched Mr. Lott walk to his car. He stopped briefly in the parking lot, and I saw that he was crying and wiping tears from his face. I suspected that he really did regret his years in the Klan; he just couldn't bring himself to admit it. There was much darkness in his past to wrestle with, more than we could talk about in the short time we had together, more than anyone would want to admit to a stranger.

To avoid embarrassing him, I waited to walk to my car until he had driven away. Our meeting had transformed Denson Lott in my mind. No longer was this man a monster who wore a white robe; he was a fellow human being who had made a decision he sorely regretted, one that pains him to this day. He deserved to be treated with dignity.

As I watched him drive away down Highway 49, I remembered that he had confirmed the identity of the black informants. Talking with either of them would no longer be possible: On an earlier visit, several months before, I had come upon my high-school friend's father's grave of freshly turned soil as I wandered through a local cemetery one day. Just as I had said a prayer of peace for that dead man whose grave I encountered, I wished that Mr. Lott might find some relief from his pain, some share of peace in this life.

TEN

True Believers

After talking with two men who fought integration, I thought it was time to interview someone on the other side of the Civil Rights movement in the 1960s. Like the old-line segregationists, many of the people on the Sovereignty Commission who could shed light on the movement perspective were dead. And as for the living, the opening of the Sovereignty Commission files had divided them, leading to accusations of personal betrayal and of the movement's goals. The files revealed that Charles Evers, Medgar's brother and one of the most visible Civil Rights activists in Mississippi in the 1960s, cooperated with the Sovereignty Commission in a manner that he likes to describe today as "negotiation." In addition, minor movement operatives were sometimes paid informants, even as they outwardly supported the movement. Add in the misinformation in the Sovereignty Commission files and disagreements over how to best open the files to the public, and things get really messy.

All the finger-pointing and accusations about who was a spy and who was not and who was a true believer in the movement or who was not made my search to find one voice from the movement difficult. But each time I searched, all the signs pointed in the direction of Ed King. Even though he, too, has been accused of betraying the movement's goals, there is no doubt in my mind that Ed King is a Civil Rights hero. His record speaks for itself.

An ordained Methodist minister and native Mississippian, Ed King immersed himself in the pursuit of racial justice in the early 1960s, a time when any white man who did so was made a social outcast as well as a target for violence. Because of his work in the Civil Rights movement, the Sovereignty Commission, along with the Citizens' Council, ran his parents out of their native Vicksburg. In his mid-twenties, in the early days of the Jackson movement, Ed King marched with Medgar Evers against segregated facilities and discriminatory practices by downtown merchants. In a funeral protest after Evers's murder, he was arrested, beaten, and thrown in a makeshift prison in a cattle stockyard on the Mississippi State Fairgrounds along with hundreds of other protesters, some of them children. In an effort to re-energize the Civil Rights movement in Mississippi, he ran as a candidate for Lieutenant Governor on the Freedom Ballot Campaign of 1963 with NAACP leader Aaron Henry on a platform calling for racial justice, school desegregation, and the right to vote. Later, along with Aaron Henry and Fannie Lou Hamer, he played an instrumental role in the establishment of the Mississippi Freedom Democratic Party, which attempted to unseat Mississippi's white establishment Democrats at the 1964 convention in Atlantic City.

Ed King paid a high price for holding to his convictions. He still bears the scars of his beatings as well as those suffered from a car collision that occurred at the height of the demonstrations in Jackson. After the accident, few in the Mississippi Civil Rights movement believed the collision was purely accidental. Today, some say he bears the psychic scars of the accident and the movement as prominently as the physical scars. Still others say that it is those psychic scars that led him to fight the full opening of the Mississippi Sovereignty Commission files, a path many characterize as misguided and an example of King's clouded judgment and betrayal of the spirit of the movement.

Rather than rely on hearsay, I decided to meet Ed King and make up my own mind. I knew that he could not change my belief that the files should be open for people of my generation to understand the injustices their parents endured and to pass that knowledge onto the next generation. After months of examining the files, I was convinced that they should be open. They revealed a concealed part of my past and shed light on a time I quickly realized I barely understood. I knew the content of the files could bring some clarity to others of my generation about those confusing times, providing a window to a culture we could not comprehend as children. However, what I did want to know was how someone who lived with the white heat of Mississippi's segregation watchdogs glaring on him could not want the inner workings of its spy agency fully exposed.

Before I met Ed King I recognized that our perspectives on life in Mississippi were completely different, and not for reasons of race. As a child, the world of hate and injustice in

Mississippi meant little to me. For the most part, my research in the Sovereignty Commission files was my first real exposure to the intensity of Mississippi's resolve to preserve a segregated society. When I was safe on my farm in Mount Olive, Ed King was fighting the Sovereignty Commission and other segregationist groups on the streets of Jackson. My experience exploring the Sovereignty Commission files was merely a baptism into that world; Ed King, however, had been washed in the blood of the Civil Rights movement.

We met in his office at the University of Mississippi Medical Center, where he teaches sociology to those studying to be physical therapists or medical technicians. As we settled into our conversation, I told him about my experiences of growing up in Mount Olive, a place where I always felt safe despite all the turmoil in Mississippi. There had been no outward black-white tension in Mount Olive, but because of the Sovereignty Commission files, I now knew of the tension that had existed below the surface, some of it generated by the Sovereignty Commission.

"Mount Olive *is* an idyllic place. That's how I remember it, too. You know, I have my own story about Mount Olive," he told me as he leaned back in his chair. This captured my attention. I wanted to hear his story.

"One morning, it was winterish I think, I had a chance to speak to a few white ministers on the Gulf Coast. Back in those days, you drove right through Mount Olive on your way to the coast. The topic of the meeting doesn't matter. It was just as good a chance as any to meet with some other white ministers who wanted the movement to succeed."

It was the fall of 1963, after the death of Medgar Evers, and the Civil Rights movement in Mississippi was losing momentum. Civil Rights workers in the state were despondent, even pessimistic, for Mississippi's authorities had tried to break the movement by jailing its leaders for anything, including phony traffic violations that required excessive bail. Ed King was chaplain at Tougaloo College, a black college outside of Jackson. He saw his meeting on the Gulf Coast as a chance to bring some other ministers into the movement's fold at a crucial point. Ed King would do anything for the movement, and that included making a 150-mile trip by himself at a time when the most recognizable white Civil Rights worker in the state could have been arrested or killed while traveling alone.

Ed left Tougaloo before dawn, before the Sovereignty Commission agents parked their cars outside the college gates to check the comings and goings of students and faculty involved in the Civil Rights movement. He traveled the back streets of Jackson to avoid running into any police or Mississippi highway patrolmen. When he reached Mount Olive undetected, he felt as if he were home free and pulled into the yard of a black church to have some coffee.

"Suddenly, I was shaking, steaming up the windows, spilling coffee from my thermos. I realized I had all this internalized fear, and that the fear had taken over me. Then I noticed that I was in Mount Olive. The religious connection hit me. Here I was scared to death in a town with a New Testament name," he said. Mount Olive was named for the very place Jesus often went for solace. Upon meditating on the significance of being so afraid in such a peaceful place, he regained his composure and continued on.

We had something in common: We had both found a safe haven in Mount Olive. Still, I had to know: Shouldn't everyone know the full story considering all the fear that had been welled up inside him during the Civil Rights movement? When historians are studying the Sovereignty Commission, trying to get a full picture of his involvement in the movement, wouldn't he want them to be able to see what information Mississippi's segregation spies kept on him? The Sovereignty Commission and other Mississippi authorities instilled crippling fear in him that morning in Mount Olive. Shouldn't they be exposed?

His answer was simple.

"The right to expose evil does not trump the right to privacy," he exclaimed gently, yet forcefully. And Ed King believes that fighting for privacy rights in the opening of the Sovereignty Commission files is an extension of his fight for fairness and democracy during the Civil Rights movement.

When historians examine the Civil Rights movement in Mississippi, Ed King wants them to identify what he actually did during the movement, not what the Sovereignty Commission said he did. From his perspective, there are far too many inaccuracies in the files for much of the information held there to be reliable for historians. "Lord help us with the errors in the files," King remarked to me with a tone of woe in his voice. What he wants to be remembered for is his contribution to change in Mississippi. That he was "accepted, trusted, tolerated, and gently educated by brothers and sisters who could see my all-American racism that I was struggling to overcome.

That may not be a visible contribution, not that a white Mississippian could change enough to be in the movement, but that I could be accepted in the movement. Helping build Freedom Summer, the Mississippi Freedom Democratic Party, those are all concrete things. But the less tangible contributions of connections to people meant more to me."

Now, many of those connections Ed King built have been severed because of his strong stance on placing privacy restrictions on the Sovereignty Commission files. Ed King did not want to block the opening of the Sovereignty Commission files; he was one of the original plaintiffs in the case calling for the opening of the files. When he joined the class-action lawsuit, he could not imagine that the files would be opened without any protection of privacy rights. He never counted on the power of pent-up grudges in Mississippi against the Sovereignty Commission to open those files at any cost. There were lots of people in Mississippi like my parents who resented paying state taxes to support being spied on. Now that those same people had a chance to blow it all open, they were going to take it.

Ed King's position was that the unlimited access I experienced during my months of research in the archives of the Sovereignty Commission might serve as a way of recirculating the Commission's smears—adding to the damage that the spying had already done to innocent people. Also, people might make assumptions that the amount of information, or the lack of information, indicated that the person under investigation had somehow served as an informant or "double agent." "There was so little in my file that was incriminating," King noted, "that some people thought my file had been purged to protect me. It was seen as proof that I had done something wrong and had something to hide."

King's situation made me think of my parents' file. I commented that in spite of my parents' involvement in voter registration and the NAACP, there was nothing incriminating in their files either. Their name was being kept there in case something did come up, and it could have been used against them. "There are people who might use that lack of evidence as a sign that they were informants," King replied. I knew for a fact that was not true. Still I knew Ed King knew what he was talking about. That accusation had been made against him for not having a file peppered with detailed references to his Civil Rights work. When Ed King moved strongly toward protecting privacy rights in the files, he was labeled as an informant, first in the idle gossip among the Mississippi Civil Rights establishment and later in the national press.

During the litigation for opening the files, there was a split among the plaintiffs. The judge divided them into what became known as the access class and the privacy class. The access class included the American Civil Liberties Union as well as a number of other plaintiffs. The privacy class included Ed King and James Salter, who was caught in the famous photograph at a Jackson lunch counter sit-in in 1963 being smeared with mustard by a mob of angry young white men. In the end, the access class won. Still the privacy class had a small victory. Before the release of the files in March 1998, the court allowed the state of Mississippi to invite people to close their files. Ads were run in local and national papers. Only forty-two people asked for their files to be protected. One of those was Ed King.

Even though he won a small victory, King feels there is still much damage done. During our talk, I quoted a remark made by Peter Maas in his reporting on the opening of the Sovereignty Commission files: "Perhaps the commission's most painful, enduring, legacy is the extent to which it has divided the civil rights community against itself—sowing seeds of suspicion and betrayal." Painfully, Ed King had to agree that the statement was accurate. "What is so ironic, is the Sovereignty Commission is dead; but it is still pushing division among those of us who needed to pass on the legacy of the Civil Rights movement." What happened to the Civil Rights community of Mississippi after the opening of the Sovereignty Commission files "is something Horace Harned and other members of the commission wish they had thought of themselves," King proclaimed with a great regret in his voice.

Although Ed King had only a pale victory in his fight to establish a right to privacy to those in the Sovereignty Commission files, he believes that there is a "great good" that has come about since they have been opened. He still wishes some individual right to privacy had been protected, and he fears that somehow, at some time years from now, the case of the opening of the Sovereignty Commission files will be used to squash privacy rights in another related circumstance. I don't know if he is right, but I see his point.

As we wrapped up our conversation, I had a flashback of sitting on the floor in front of our black-and-white console television in Mount Olive watching the local news from WLBT in Jackson. Whenever I saw news of Civil Rights marches in Jackson, there was a sea of black men and women. In the background was a lone white man in a clerical collar. No one ever said who he was or why he was there; I just assumed that he was one of those Northern whites I read about in scathing articles in the *Clarion-Ledger* about Civil Rights protests. He always tended to stand in the background, rarely in front, when the camera came in his direction. Little did I know that, like me, he was a local person, born and raised in Mississippi. As a young man he left Mississippi, but he came back. He could have stayed away, yet he made a conscious choice to come back at a time of great struggle and upheaval. And he chose to stand on the front lines, albeit in the background lest he be accused of being a white man who wanted to tell black people the best way to gain their freedom.

When Ed King was growing up, people who did not fit in down in Mississippi had to leave. You either accepted the status quo, or you left. When you left, you became what King calls an "intellectual or spiritual refugee." As a minister, Ed King would have been a spiritual refugee, but he chose not to be one. He believed that you had to live out your spiritual life in the world; and you can't be separated from the place you came from. So, Ed King came back and fought to make Mississippi a better place, in spite of being ostracized by his family and cast out by his colleagues in the clergy.

Even though King tells me with a tinge of sadness in his voice that "My reputation will never be recovered," I know he believes the fight was worth it. That's what it takes to be a true believer. You must never give up the fight.

Part FOUR

Reconciliation

❖   ❖   ❖

. . . the South, with all the monstrous mythologizing of its virtues, nevertheless has these virtues — a manner and a grace and a gift for human intercourse.
—Walker Percy, from "Mississippi: The Fallen Paradise"

ELEVEN

A Trusty Compass

After my father's death, I vowed that I would never return to our farm. On visit after visit to Mississippi over the years, I avoided even driving by the house, taking detours down winding country roads just so I wouldn't have to see it and could keep my memories intact. But the more I spent time in Mississippi as I explored the Sovereignty Commission files, the more I felt pulled back to the old home place. Part of me said that a trip back to where I began would help ease the pain of seeing what had happened to Mount Olive, or at least put it in perspective. Or maybe it would help me make sense of everything I had experienced as I studied report after report in the Sovereignty Commission files.

The pull back to my farm began in Jackson in the reading room of the Mississippi Department of Archives and History soon after I began my research in the Sovereignty Commission files. As I browsed through a miscellaneous manuscript file labeled "Mount Olive, Covington County," I came upon a newspaper article reporting the destruction of a home by a tornado in 1992. From what I read, I was certain it was my old house. The article described a house on Highway 35 outside of Mount Olive that looked as if it had been "trampled." Suddenly I recalled that a family friend had used the exact same words about the destruction. After hours of poring over more Sovereignty Commission documents, I went back to the article and read it again. Convinced now that this yellowed news clipping was a sign that I had to go see what was left of my old house, I photocopied the piece, packed my research in my backpack, and started driving south to Mount Olive. I reassured myself on the hour-long drive that after a brief walk around town, as I did on many a Saturday afternoon as a child, I would muster up the courage to pay the place a visit. This visit would be different. My life had changed a great deal since I last saw the farm.

The last time I had visited the farm was a month after my father had died. Although my family had sold the farm in 1974, two years before his death, I drove there from Oxford on Good Friday of 1976, thinking that the place he loved and built into a thing of beauty would somehow lessen my grief. But time was starting to take its toll; the farm was looking shabby and unkempt, with overgrown fields filled with weeds and an overgrown lawn. The place no longer resembled the farm of my childhood, with its tidy green lawn, peach orchard set in the field of red clover, and rolling pastures. On that spring afternoon, I just lay on the uneven lawn and wept.

"This time will be different," I said to myself. "I can keep my emotions in check." I was no longer a grief-stricken teenager; I was a settled, stable, middle-aged man. Plus, since the town that I remembered had changed so radically, I could certainly handle seeing what had happened to my farm.

When I drove up the hill to the site of my old house and farm, I avoided looking at where the house had once stood. I hastily parked the car in the field across the road, which my father had called "the front forty," and got out to take a look.

A barren chinaberry tree, the same one I had climbed as a boy, loomed over the driveway, which still had gravel but was spotted with tall blades of grass. I glanced across the road from the same spot that I picked up our mail each day after school. As my eyes soaked in the familiar view, I saw that all that remained of the house was a concrete slab of a carport and a small section of the walkway where I had learned to ride a bicycle. A makeshift carport had been built over the slab and a trailer placed beside it that covered part of the walkway.

I knocked on the door of the trailer to see if anyone was home. When no one answered, I stood back and looked at the spot where my house had once stood. Tears flowed down my face, just as they had when I visited the farm after my father died.

I vowed years ago to never return to this spot. Why did I come?

I closed my eyes and everything came back to me: the brick and white clapboard house, the neatly trimmed rows of boxwoods. It was springtime; the peach orchard to my right smelled fragrant with blossoms and was filled with red clover. The rose garden was just to my left; I could see the tin roof of the barn off in the distance. I heard the sound of my father on his tractor and my sisters inside the house arguing about who was to wash or dry the dishes. My dog, Blondie, was barking and chasing a crop-dusting plane. I could hear my mother twang, "At least it won't hit her and kill her like a truck would."

I opened my eyes. It was all gone. I was standing in front of another tacky trailer in Mississippi.

Suddenly I knew why I had come back: to connect with the past, to give meaning to the present. Everything that little farm in Mississippi ever was, or meant, was still inside of me. It has always been and always would be. The most powerful storm could never take away the love that grew there. I was standing on the ground of my old home place, but its spirit lived inside of me.

I wiped my face with my hands and went back to the car where I sat and listened to the hovering silence, broken by the occasional truck driving past on the highway, a sound I knew from when I was a boy. I remembered wandering the hills of the farm and dreaming of going far away from this place to a big city like New York or London, or any of the cities whose clear-channel radio stations I listened to on a tiny green transistor radio under my covers at night. I wondered if there were still little boys and girls living on isolated farms like this one who dreamed of what it would be like to visit the faraway places they read about in books and magazines. Were there people to tell those dreamy, wide-eyed boys and girls that anything is possible, even in Mississippi, just as my parents and teachers had told me?

I thought about what had happened to all the people I grew up with, as well as all those who had opened their doors to me when I sat at their tables as the county agent's son. Some of them were dreamers like me. Others, like many black Mississippians, had little room for hopes or dreams but dreamed anyway. Were they still here?

As I drove away I knew what I had to do. I had to find out if the strength and joy I had carried away from Mount Olive was still here.

In the months that followed, I returned to the site of my old house on several occasions. No longer did its almost total disappearance torment me. Each time, being on the spot helped me think through what I had discovered about Mississippi and myself. Like the day I first came back to find a trailer on the site, I didn't always like what I found.

My routine in visiting the house was often the same: I parked across the road, stared across at the spot, and sometimes walked around my old yard. I always knocked on the door of the trailer to let whoever lived there know of my presence. Though I heard sounds inside, no one ever answered the door.

One spring day as I was walking around the old yard, I wondered if I embraced the memory of this place so intensely that I could see little else: The myth of the place had become stronger than the reality. The emotional barriers created by the myth had kept me from anticipating the chilly reception my wife Colleen and I had received just twelve years before. The forces of the myth had also made me hesitate to return to Mississippi to delve into the Sovereignty Commission and Mississippi's place, exposing me to a far more complex world in Mississippi than the one I wanted to know.

On another one of my solitary walks around my old farm, I pondered why I sometimes felt like an outsider in Mississippi both while growing up here and later as an adult. In the three years since coming back to Mississippi, that feeling had largely left me. Was that a myth, too? When my family lived on our farm, we were outsiders by virtue of the circumstances of our birth and where we chose to live. That was clear to me from conversations I had as I traveled around on my visits back to Mount Olive. My family held that outsider status almost like a badge of honor, if only as a means to push us out into a wider world. The outsider label stuck with me, since I felt that I did not belong in Mount Olive all through my high-school years. I had carried it away with me when I left Mississippi and held onto it. But the people of Mount Olive helped me throw away my outsider status.

All of Mount Olive knew that I was plundering around in the Sovereignty Commission files, looking for ties to Mount Olive. I made no secret of what I had come back searching for. Still, no one ever discouraged me or spoke disparagingly about what I was doing. In my exchanges with people, I could tell they were being sincere, not just polite and mannerly. When I knew that I could tell the difference, I began to feel like a native, and my status as an outsider largely shattered. For the first time in my life, I felt as if Mount Olive was a place where I belonged. And some of the people whom I thought would treat me like an outsider happened to be the ones who gave me the strongest sense of belonging.

My old house acted as a compass for me to find my direction, since each time I delved into the files I found myself immersed in a past that I did not recognize. Coming back to the spot where my old house had stood helped me connect with that past and see it more realistically, not through the romantic lens that had often clouded my perspective. Sometimes as I stood on the spot where my farm had once stood, I remembered snippets of the world that had passed by on Highway 35, people and events that seemed routine as a child but now mean more: visits from Mr. Rutland, the highway patrolman cited in the Sovereignty Commission files of registering blacks to vote, or the sight of a sheriff's car driving slowly by as I played in the yard. The day I read the report from the county sheriff noting that, although he could not put his finger on any NAACP member in his county, he was of the opinion that there were a number of NAACP members who were "acting in a very quiet manner in Covington County," I found myself driving up the hill to my farm to think. In the quiet of that country road, I remembered how the sheriff sometimes drove by our place when I was a boy. Though I thought it was normal at the time, I am now certain that his observations were being made for a completely different reason. How could they not be? Also, there were the hang-up phone calls we would get with some regularity. These insights brought on a more intense feeling in me, a conviction that there was more in the files about my parents and that it had been destroyed. There was no way for me to prove that of course. Suddenly, the inclusion of my parents' names in the files made sense to me and seemed less arbitrary. Yes, there was much I would never know, but there was also much I had discovered.

I had learned that in Mississippi the forces of the past are alive and the ghosts of the past live on in the present. Whether

I was in the archives studying the Sovereignty Commission files or on the site of my old house, I felt the urgent presence of those ghosts. On each trip back to Mississippi, I now willingly stared them in the face. I had to. I kept coming back to face them because I knew that that was the only way I could ever know what Mississippi was really like. And that was why I had come back in the first place.

What is Mississippi like? It's a volatile world with dizzyingly complex social and cultural layers; as I visited more and more, I became accustomed to navigating my way through this tangled world where the past and the present and the sacred and the profane exist side by side. Rather than questioning its complexities, I accepted them. To accept them, I had to toss aside the romantic notions I had of Mississippi. I began at the place in Mississippi that meant the most to me: my old farm.

Even with the moments of clarity about Mississippi that I grasped on my walks around my old farm, I had trouble accepting that my home was gone. The ghosts of the past dogged me. Each time I returned home to Washington from Mississippi, I had the same dream: The house was back on its original spot and everything was just the way it was when I was a child. In that dream, I owned the house and had restored it to a splendor that I admit it never had, but seemed vaguely familiar. Each time I awakened with a tranquil, confused feeling; there was something different about the house, but I couldn't put my finger on it. Sometimes, I tried to figure out what was different and what was so comforting. Even though the house was still located on the same spot in Mississippi, some things in it had changed. Early one morning after one of my dreams, I paced my house in Washington and suddenly it hit me: The interior of the house in my dream was actually my house in Washington. The rooms I wandered though in my dream were the rooms of my house, only relocated on the spot of the old home place in Mississippi.

When I realized how much I had melded the past into the present, I stopped having the dream. My house in Washington was my real home. That piece of Mississippi ground outside Mount Olive bore no signs of my presence and no longer belonged to me. That spot is merely a memory, the thing of dreams and wishes that can't come true. After coming to that realization, I let go of a piece of my past.

TWELVE

Goin' Down South

Three years passed from when we had our first bedtime conversation about Mississippi to when my sons, Patrick and Aidan, and I made our first visit there. In spite of the years of my telling them stories about Mississippi, it existed in their imaginations less as a real place and more as an idea. Both Patrick and Aidan knew that I had been traveling there to find out why the state had spied on their grandparents and people like them. Somehow, in their little boy minds, a place that spied on people couldn't be real; spying happened only in the movies, not to real people. The specter of spying and deceit added to the air of mystery they felt about Mississippi, which they shared with me whenever we talked about a trip there.

"They don't spy on people down there anymore, do they?" Aidan asked me one night. I reassured him that things were different now and that when we finally did make our trip there together nothing like that would happen to us.

Though I had come to see Mississippi in a way that I thought was clearer, more realistic than it was the night I lay next to them in their beds and struggled with what to tell them about my home state, I shared little of what I had discovered in the years that followed. Something inside begged me not to intrude too much on what Patrick and Aidan would see when they finally visited Mississippi. Just as I constructed my own sense of Mississippi as a child, and a different concept of it as an adult, I knew their visit should be a time for them to find a vision of the place that belonged only to them. My job had to be limited to showing them the landscape; only they could choose what to paint.

Each time I returned to Mississippi, I wrestled with Patrick and Aidan's question of when they would accompany me on a trip to this distant, mysterious place. "Dad needs to finish his work there before you can come," I would always tell them. "Oh, the spying," Aidan said to me, an air of disappointment in his voice one night before I left. Though they were clearly disappointed, my answer satisfied them. However, as time went by, they were not so accepting. Their requests to travel with me became more pointed, direct, and demanding. They sensed that I was holding something back from them, something special that belonged to them. And I was. They were ready, but I was not.

Late one spring afternoon, as I drove down a long flat stretch of Interstate 55, watching the sun set on a broad span of Delta land, I heard my sons' voices making their plea. Maybe something in the scenery spoke to me; the starkness of the Delta can be described in words, but it is best to witness it in person. It wasn't fair to keep this scene to myself, one I had shared so many times with my own father as we drove south toward

Mount Olive after trekking around the Delta. Now I enjoyed it alone, and it didn't feel right. It was then that I made up my mind, and as soon as I could, I called home. "We'll take a trip to Mississippi for your spring break," I said, speaking into a crackly cellular phone first to Patrick, then Aidan. I could hear their broad smiles on the other end of the phone.

"Are you sure about this?" my wife Colleen asked, as the phone was passed back to her. I knew that she couldn't bear the thought of her children facing the rejection we felt when we first visited Mississippi together in 1990. Quickly I assured her that I was very sure; at that moment, I could not have been more sure. From the tone of my voice, she could tell that I was ready for this trip and that my journey back to Mississippi had reached a different stage. She was right. It had.

The trip I was then on marked two years of digging into the soul of Mississippi's darker side; I was ready to move on. My voyage back had begun with memories, then moved into the actual past as a way to fill in the gaps the mind chooses to neglect and ignore. No longer did I feel that I had run away from one side of my past, nor did I feel encumbered by it. As I experienced the spare beauty of Mississippi the place that day, I felt bathed in its light and unburdened; I wanted to walk in that same light with my children.

A few days after my phone call, I returned home. Greeting me in our living room was a stack of books checked out from our local library on Mississippi, tagged with a list of "must see" attractions, such as ancient Indian mounds, sacred sites of the blues, the Vicksburg Civil War Battlefield, and the Natchez

Trace. Patrick and Aidan had already begun to find the scenery for their landscape.

A month later, on Easter Sunday, our week-long Southern travel odyssey began in an old Volvo station wagon with a yellow-highlighted map directing our route and the North Mississippi All-Stars version of R.L. Burnside's "Shake 'em on Down" propelling us southward toward Mississippi. It was a boys' road trip; after twelve years, Colleen still could not bring herself to return. "Everyone should see Mississippi at least once, and I've done that," she assured Patrick and Aidan. "This is a special trip for you to enjoy just with Dad." Five-year-old Delaney looked at us wistfully as we pulled away, a look on her face that said, "When will it be my turn?" Sooner rather than later, I thought to myself.

Patrick and Aidan yearned to see the Delta and the places they read about in their assorted collection of books, but we could only make it as far as the hills of eastern Tennessee on our first day out. Southern lore says that the Mississippi Delta begins in the lobby of the Peabody Hotel in Memphis and ends on Catfish Row in Vicksburg. I told them that the next day, when we arrived in Memphis, our trip to Mississippi would officially begin. By early afternoon, we were gazing on the Mississippi River from the bluffs of Memphis and strolling down Beale Street.

Though I wanted Patrick and Aidan to see Mississippi through their own eyes, I just couldn't hold back the urge to show them the world of my childhood. The Mississippi I knew as a child existed in the files of the Sovereignty Commission and in the pages of history books. Our trip had to reveal to them that the freedom to explore Mississippi without barriers had come at a price. So, after a quick walk on Beale Street, I gave them a glimpse into the segregated South, the one they had only seen in books. We strolled over to see the National Civil Rights Museum at the Lorraine Motel, where there is a timeline in the exhibits that served as the backdrop of my childhood. Before I left them to form their own impressions of the South, they had to see that part of my history, which was their history as well.

As we walked through the exhibits, I showed them places they would see as we traveled through Mississippi: Delta shacks, the Lyceum building at Ole Miss, the bus station in downtown Jackson, where the Freedom Riders arrived. In one room filled with televisions showing footage of events from the Civil Rights era, I found Aidan fixated on a screen.

"Who is that man, and what happened to his face?" he asked bluntly.

"That's Ed King, someone Dad talked to for his work. His face was scarred from a car accident. And that's Fannie Lou Hamer sitting beside him. She worked hard for the right for black people in the Mississippi Delta to vote. Maybe we can see Mr. King in a few days and he can tell you all about her." Aidan took that as an acceptable answer and we moved on through the exhibit.

As we watched screen after screen, many of the scenes of Civil Rights events frightened both boys to the point that they visibly grimaced at the sight of angry mobs and dogs and hoses being turned on black children and adults. As they stood soaking up these moments of terror, I flashed back to the time I saw these very same scenes. It didn't take much, since I saw the same fear I felt welling up in their eyes. The only difference in our reactions was the effect of time: When I first saw these images, the events were actually happening; my sons were seeing them recorded on tape in a museum. Upon sensing their discomfort, I reassured them that it was all over; it was history now. But that did not quell their fears. The black-and-white news footage seemed as real to them as it had to me when I was their age. We did not linger to capture every nuance of the era. I knew how those images made a child feel insecure, planting the thoughts that someone could randomly commit a violent act against your family or even against you. They wanted to move on, and we did.

The exhibit ended at the balcony of rooms 306 and 307, where Martin Luther King was assassinated. As we stood looking at the rooms as they were left on April 4, 1968, Aidan asked me if we could leave. He wouldn't cry, but clearly being in those rooms troubled him; he knew a man had been murdered only several feet away. Patrick, on the other hand, resolved to read with dogged determination every panel in the exhibit. Aidan and I left him there, the strains of Mahalia Jackson singing "Precious Lord, Take My Hand" filling the space outside.

Outside that room in the Lorraine Motel, I gave my best effort to get Aidan to talk to me about what scared him. Nothing could coax him into admitting any fear whatsoever. He stood beside me in stern, stoic silence. My mind raced as we waited there and I hoped I had not wrecked the trip for him by intruding on his impressions and bringing him to a place marked by violence. Minutes later, he seemed to have recovered completely.

Patrick made it off the Lorraine Motel balcony, and our visit took a more lighthearted turn. We looked in the shop windows on Beale Street, visited the lobby of Peabody Hotel, and drove by Sun Records, where Elvis Presley made his first record. The next day, we took a trip to Graceland. The pure kitsch of the mansion and the famous pink Cadillac in the Elvis Presley Automobile Museum put the rest of the trip on a more upbeat note.

It was on to the Delta and as we drove down Highway 61, Patrick and Aidan stared out the windows with awe at the spare, flat Mississippi Delta landscape: the cotton fields, the catfish ponds, with the billboards advertising riverboat gambling and casinos along the Mississippi River. This time, we were headed to a spot they wanted to visit, rather than one selected by their dad: Moorhead, Mississippi, where the Southern and the Yellow Dog railroad lines meet at a perfectly perpendicular crossing. The boys read in one of their books on Mississippi that John Henry, the steel-driving man of American folk legend, built the Yellow Dog railroad. A picture of John Henry had hung in their room all of their lives, so this somehow made that image of John Henry sitting on the railroad tracks with his hammer in his hand seem real. Then, before we left for Mississippi, they heard these lines from a blues song on a radio program one afternoon:

Said Southern cross the dog at Moorhead,
     mama, Lord, and
She keeps on through
I say my baby's gone to Georgia, I believe
     I'll go to Georgia too.

The rhythm of that song stuck with them; plus the name was something so foreign to them, they had to see it. Unlike the Crossroads in Clarksdale, where Robert Johnson allegedly made his legendary deal with the devil, I had never been to where the Southern crosses the Dog. So it seemed like a perfect place for us to experience together.

On our way to Moorhead, we drove through the Crossroads up in Clarksdale. But I didn't ask Patrick and Aidan to fall down on their knees and ask the Lord to have mercy on them, if he pleased. I just pointed out the landmark and headed straight to Moorhead, just as they asked me to do.

We pulled into Moorhead just before twilight, and the Delta sun glistened on the railroad tracks and all that surrounded the barren town with its shuttered storefronts. "Is this a ghost town, Dad?" they asked matter of factly. "No," I told them. "This is just an old Delta town down on its luck." The money that built Moorhead grew on cotton stalks, and now there's simply not much money in cotton anymore.

For the next hour, we teetered around on the tracks of the Southern and Yellow Dog railroads, balancing one foot in front of the other and reveling in the failing Delta twilight. I don't know what Patrick and Aidan were thinking, but as I looked at the intersection of these two railroads, straighter than the Crossroads we came through to get here, I knew that I had come to another crossroads of my own. It took hold of me and pushed me up on my feet rather than to my knees. The blues that had filled my head as we drove through the Delta left me, and I enjoyed this moment in a place that had somehow summoned me there to experience this very feeling. As night fell, I had to press the boys to leave Moorhead behind and head further south, away from the Delta, through many of the same towns their grandparents left behind more than forty years ago.

After showing them Jackson and Vicksburg, the time came for us to spend a day in Mount Olive, a place we all wanted to see together. Patrick and Aidan were eager to see where I went to school and played as a boy, even though I warned them that there really wasn't that much to see of the Mount Olive I knew as a child. My warnings meant nothing, as they saw this visit almost as an archeological expedition to find the remains of a place their father once knew.

We drove down Main Street and then parked by Mount Olive High School, where we walked the halls. I showed Patrick and Aidan a place I had largely chosen to forget: all the classrooms I spent time in, the room where their grandmother taught fifth grade, the gym where my graduation ceremony was held, which, before visiting there with my sons was the only happy day I remember during my years in school at Mount Olive High School. Attentively, they took in all the sights I pointed out. Then Patrick said, "Dad, this is just an old school; can we go see the town?"

There wasn't much of the old Mount Olive left to see, but we headed to the one place in Mount Olive that had changed the least: Powell's Drug Store. The comic book rack I loved was gone, but I knew that the soda fountain with an old-fashioned box filled with icy-cold bottles of Coca-Cola was still there. As we walked in, Homer Powell greeted us. "It's so good to see y'all. Are these your boys? They sure are fine-looking boys. What can I do for y'all today?"

"We want a Coca-Cola in a bottle," Patrick and Aidan announced. Everyone in the drugstore chuckled audibly at the request. I explained that they had never had a Coke in an old-fashioned bottle and had been looking for one since we left Washington. Even the original Coca-Cola factory over in Vicksburg, which they had chosen to visit for that very reason, didn't have them. Powell's was the place that I knew would have icy-cold Cokes just as I remembered them; I had stopped here for one on every trip to Mount Olive I had made over the past few years. Mrs. Powell went behind the soda fountain and pulled out three cokes for us, and Patrick and Aidan happily began to guzzle them down, staring at the bottles with wonderment. Mr. and Mrs. Powell laughed, enjoying the uniqueness of something we all took for granted.

After we left, we walked around town and I took them on my old rounds, the one I took whenever I came to town as a boy: We went to Boxx's service station, where the Green Tree Hotel once stood, as well as my cherished old phone booth. The service station was abandoned now, but seemed fixed in time, with an old black 1962 Ford Galaxie parked outside by the service bay that could have been there when I was a boy. We went to Polk and Ducksworth's Feed Mill, the fire station, and up and down Main Street.

Patrick and Aidan saw that there really wasn't that much in the town of Mount Olive and told me they wanted to see my old farm. "There's even less to see there," I told them, reminding them of the tornado that had destroyed everything I had once known. They didn't seem to mind. They wanted to see what was left, just as they had seen what was left of downtown Mount Olive.

As we returned to our car, with the Coca-Cola bottles held tightly in Patrick and Aidan's hands as cherished souvenirs, a familiar sound came through town: I looked up and saw a shining engine of the Illinois Central headed down the railroad tracks. I had seen that same sight as a boy. At that moment, I knew that even though there wasn't much left in Mount Olive from my days, Patrick and Aidan had now gotten the full experience of my old Saturday trip to town. And I had, too. As I stood by the car, smiling broadly as I watched the train rumble by, the sound of the train whistle filled my mind with pictures of those days. Lost in a reverie that seemed like a few seconds to me, Patrick emitted an impatient yell.

"Why are you just standing there? Can we go now?" he shouted.

Though I wanted to watch the train pull out of sight, at Patrick and Aidan's urging we moved down Main Street to Highway 35 bound for my old home place. As was now my custom, I parked across the road from the trailer and went and knocked on the door. As always, no one answered. So, completely on our own, we began to take a look around together.

Both boys stared with disbelief that such a stark setting could ever have been lush and vibrant. To pierce their silence, I began to tell them where everything once stood as we moved around the old yard: the chinaberry tree, the orchard, the barn, and the path where I learned to ride a bicycle. Together, we climbed my old chinaberry tree, still the only remnant standing of my home. Its branches were not the same ones I knew, for they now grew from the stump of the tree that had been there, obviously another casualty of the tornado. That didn't matter to them; it was the one thing I remembered that was left, and they were glad it was there.

Later we walked around to the back of the trailer, where there stood an old shed that, judging from the age of the wood and tin, had been constructed from the remains of our old barn. At the shed, we tried to look down the hill at what we had called the "back 40," where the brook and Turtle Ridge were two places I had told Patrick and Aidan about many times. Thinking of the small toy boat they had in the back of the car, the boys wanted to blaze a trail through the brush down to those places. I knew that they were far too overgrown to be enjoyed, except in my memories. Much to their disappointment, I insisted that we stay on what was once my old yard.

This was the first visit to the old home place where I felt upbeat and not saddened by what had once been there. The sounds of my children playing in the same spot where I played made what seemed like a lonely wasteland come alive. Together we walked and I told stories about things I did as a boy and where I did them: playing war with chinaberries; damming up muddy streams and sliding down hills in wet clothes while sitting in a cardboard box; and the intense joys I felt running across the road to get the mail, especially when I was expecting a letter from the many pen pals who served as my window to a world beyond these hills. Before we left, Patrick looked at me with a drawn look of disappointment on his face.

"Does it make you sad to come here? " he asked.

"No, Patrick, not anymore," I told him. "This place doesn't belong to me anymore. It's not my home. It was a long time ago, but it's not anymore. And that's ok."

Although I could tell from the expression on his face that he did not understand what I meant, I knew that he would someday, just as I finally understood what my father said to me on our last walk together on this same spot. One day Patrick would realize that some places belong only to the ages and memory; they are best enjoyed that way, rather than forcing their re-creation in a world where they no longer fit into lives that were formed by those very places. Once the mourning for what once was or might have been is over, life can move on. Though I thought I had moved on before now, after my talk with Patrick I was certain that I had.

After we left my old farm, with the afternoon falling into the dimming of another day in Mississippi, we spent the rest of our time in and around Mount Olive just driving down country roads, stopping wherever looked interesting to them: the general store in Hot Coffee, a llama farm on the Sunset Road near Collins, and a grassy bank along the Okatoma Creek, where we pitched rocks. We stayed in Mount Olive well until nightfall.

After the years of feeling fear and foreboding about Mississippi, I felt filled with joy and wonder about the place, as I had as a boy. The edginess I always thought I would have coming here with my sons never overtook me. Had I changed or had the place changed? I didn't know which. I just enjoyed the moment.

Fathers often tell their sons things that they want them to learn on their own or plant coded advice in their consciousness. But after leaving Mount Olive they turned the tables on me and taught me a thing or two about letting go of the past. We had driven to Oxford and after a guided tour of Oxford and Ole Miss by my former German professor, Ron Bartlett, we visited the Lyceum building. During our visit to the chancellor's office, the boys were given a choice of Ole Miss hats: one white, without the team name Rebels emblazoned on it, and one bright red and blue, with "Rebels" on the back. In my time at Ole Miss, I refused to wear anything that said Rebels or bore a caricature of the team mascot, Colonel Rebel.

Of course, they chose the red hat, with Rebels stitched on the back. What kid wouldn't want a bright red hat?

As we walked through the Lyceum doors, the very same doors through which James Meredith entered Ole Miss forty years before, Aidan asked me, perhaps sensing my discomfort, "Is this a bad name on this hat? Should we go back and get the white hat?"

I reassured him and Patrick that by choosing the red hat that they had not done a bad thing or that the hat was marked with an offensive name. "Ole Miss's team is called the Rebels," I told them. Quickly, into my field of vision came the red brick spire of Ventress Hall. I remembered that one wall of Ventress Hall held a Louis Comfort Tiffany stained-glass window depicting the Ole Miss University Greys in battle during the Civil War. I could reassure them that the name on their hat was tied to the history of Ole Miss, whether I subscribed to that history or not. So we strolled down University Circle to the edge of the Grove for a little history lesson.

Once inside Ventress Hall, I was struck by the beauty of the window, in spite of the romanticized vision it depicted of noble men battling for "Southern independence," as I had been taught at Mount Olive High School. As we looked at the window together, studied it, discussed the battle scene, and talked about the different ways people remember the Civil War, this piece of Ole Miss history became a part of my history. During my time at Ole Miss, I had fought a number of battles; unlike the University Greys, I prevailed, since I was standing there with my children. And my sons represented the future rather than a lost cause from the past. So, at a memorial to the men of the Confederacy, I finally became an Ole Miss Rebel myself, but on my terms.

We were finishing up our tour of Ventress Hall when William Winter, a former governor of Mississippi, walked into the building. I introduced myself and reminded him that he had spoken at my high school graduation. Like any good politician, he indicated some vague memory of having given a commencement address in Mount Olive, Mississippi, in 1974.

In all my research into the Sovereignty Commission files, William Winter's name stood out as the one Mississippi politician who disapproved of its work. Winter was one of only twenty-three members of the Mississippi House of Representatives who voted against the formation of the Sovereignty Commission in 1956, rightly fearing that money from the Commission would end up in the hands of the Citizens' Council. As Lieutenant Governor in 1972, though he made appointments to the Sovereignty Commission, he never attended a meeting. "Advice as to whether you will be with us will be genuinely appreciated," Sovereignty Commission chair Webb Burke wrote to Winter as a plea to attend one of the last meetings before the governor shut the Sovereignty Commission down. Winter's stance on race hurt him politically, and he was only elected governor in 1980, a time when politics in the state had begun to move beyond race. As a former governor, he advocated a new state flag and headed up a racial reconciliation group in the state. If there was one Mississippi politician I wanted my sons to meet, it was William Winter. And he embraced them as if they were his own.

Governor Winter had come to Ole Miss to speak to new members of Phi Beta Kappa. For years, Ole Miss had been unable to secure a Phi Beta Kappa chapter, and now it is the first public college in the state to have its own chapter of the prestigious academic honorary. As always, Governor Winter spoke to the future of Mississippi. In particular, he spoke to me of the future of Ole Miss and urged me to rise to the challenge of making Mississippi a great place. After my talk with Governor Winter and the realization that we were both in Oxford on a significant day in Ole Miss's history, I put the bright red Ole Miss Rebels hats firmly on Patrick and Aidan's heads and told them to wear them with pride. Though mine did not say Rebels, I wore my hat proudly as well.

As the day wore on, the time came for us to leave our Mississippi odyssey. When we started our drive back to Washington that night, we talked about the trip and all the places we had been, as well as a few places on their list we had not gotten to see. We agreed that this trip to Mississippi would not be their last; there would be other trips, and we would get to see those things and a few places they had not even thought of. Then I asked them what they thought about Mississippi.

What they enjoyed the most were the places we visited that seemed to be frozen in time: the general store in Hot Coffee, where a bag full of candy could be had for a mere 88 cents; the almost prehistoric look of the Delta landscape; our playing Civil War soldiers on the battlefield in Vicksburg; climbing trees and rolling down the green hills of a friend's Covington County farm, hills that I told them looked like the ones behind my old house before they became overgrown. They liked that every day had been an adventure, one often accompanied by rough play in grass and mud.

They seemed wistful and sad that our trip was over. The car became quiet, then Patrick decided to break the silence.

"Dad," Patrick said, "Mississippi is a very cool place."

I was stunned. That's not how I thought of Mississippi. As a child I thought of Mississippi as the most uncool place on the planet, particularly compared with the world beyond its borders. My mind flashed back to all those letters I had written to childhood pen pals in England, Australia, and New Zealand. These missives were often punctuated with my despair about how dull and ordinary the life I led in rural Mississippi must seem to them compared with growing up in London, Melbourne, or Auckland. In my mind, those were the cool places, not Mississippi.

Patrick's comment had jolted me, and I didn't respond in any significant way, nor did I think I should. As we drove away from Mississippi, into the deep pitch black of a Tennessee night, I kept saying to myself, like a mantra, "Mississippi is a very cool place."

Before the night was over, I didn't have to say it anymore. I believed it.

Epilogue

Return to a Very Cool Place

Distance has its own way of creating a sense of intimacy. Whether people or places are near or far from us lands them in our hearts in unexpected ways and sometimes draws us closer to them. It was distance that drew me closer to Mississippi.

I thought the years of distance I placed between myself and Mississippi would make it easier for me to peer into a time during which I was nurtured into adulthood in one of its small towns. Distance, coupled with the passage of time, would keep me safe from Mississippi's siren call, a call to which I thought I had built up a resistance. The more I learned about the era of the Sovereignty Commission in Mississippi, the more I expected that distance would grow, allowing me to remain detached from the place. But as I drew Mississippi closer to examine both the good and the bad, I could no longer keep it shut away in the part of myself that would analyze it, examine it, and place it off in the distance. Every inch of Mississippi became a part of me again. It got under my skin, not just in my head.

On each successive trip back to Mississippi, I found out more and more about how the whole state was torn asunder by the forces of race and hate, with its government prodding those forces into open battle. People were murdered, property was destroyed, and lives were wrecked beyond recognition. In time, I encountered people who were caught in the forces of this battle for the soul of Mississippi, and their stories sometimes moved me to anger and rage. I didn't plan on falling in love with a place that would make me clench my fists and grit my teeth. But once I understood Mississippi's past in my head, I could find a place for it in my heart.

Closing the distance from the place nurtured a love for Mississippi that I had hiding inside me, a love that made my remoteness crumble. Admittedly, Mississippi's not an easy place to love, and I've witnessed firsthand how its charms can be fleeting. Confronting its many imperfections, rather than hiding from them, made it easier to love. And I discovered that it is Mississippi's complicated imperfections that make it such a cool place.

Staring down Mississippi's imperfections also gave me a greater appreciation for my parents' courage. Finally, I caught a glimpse of the world they struggled through and saw how hard they had to work to keep the negative side of Mississippi from seeping into the lives of their children. I realized why my mother could not explain this to me in words. To understand this, you had to live it. As I paged through the files, for the first time I shared some of the anger and pain she and my father must have felt. And it is because of what they went through that I could find a way to love Mississippi today.

The night I first saw my parents' names on the Sovereignty Commission list, I felt no love for Mississippi, only repulsion for a place that would spy on its own citizens. Yet it was by exploring the very forces that sickened me that I came to see how Mississippi is struggling toward redemption from its dark period. Witnessing those forces of redemption at work in the people of Mississippi brought me closer to Mississippi in a way that was unimaginable just a short time ago.

The forces of redemption in Mississippi began with the reopening of one of the Civil Rights era's most cold-blooded murders. And it was evidence from Mississippi's spy agency, leaked to Jackson *Clarion-Ledger* reporter Jerry Mitchell, that led to the discovery that the state of Mississippi had obstructed justice in the murder case of Medgar Evers. Those leaked documents not only led to the retrial and conviction of Byron de la Beckwith, the man who murdered Evers, but also to the opening of the Sovereignty Commission files, laying the unspoken deeds of the past out in the open. In turn, the opening of the Sovereignty Commission brought about a more open dialogue among the people of Mississippi about the struggle for equality fought by its black citizens. The active role of the state of Mississippi in maintaining segregation could no longer be dismissed as hearsay. There were documents to prove it.

In a conversation I had with Jerry Mitchell, he affirmed his belief that the opening of the Sovereignty Commission files, coupled with the reopening of the Medgar Evers murder case, spawned a national movement that has led to the reinvestigation of twenty-two deaths from the Civil Rights era and to twenty-four arrests as a consequence. Of those arrests, there have been sixteen convictions, two acquittals, and one mistrial. According to Jerry, these arrests, retrials, and convictions represent "the nation's Nuremberg for the unpunished crimes of the Civil Rights era." Mark Potok of the Civil Rights advocacy group Klanwatch has called these "atonement trials." No matter what you call them, once they began, nothing in Mississippi could be the same.

Civil Rights–era historian John Dittmer agrees. "The Evers trial was a catalyst for the movement toward atonement trials. There would have been some need for atonement, regardless of the opening of the Sovereignty Commission files, but that event definitely speeded things along." Dittmer also views the Sovereignty Commission files as a significant cultural phenomenon of recent American history from which we can still draw some lessons. "Nationally we are moving more to these situations where people can investigate with impunity, and people feel threatened by it. We must not move back to what Mississippi used to be."

Though Mississippi is not the same place it used to be, the forces of its darker era still rise up and make themselves known. There are no longer secret investigations and informants, but the coded speech once used by the Sovereignty Commission is still at work in Mississippi and plays a role in daily life. I've heard it in politicians' speeches, seen it on a campaign sign dubbing a candidate as "one of us, for all of us" and read it in letters written to the editor of the *Clarion-Ledger* about race relations.

Senator Trent Lott even fell into Mississippi's coded political speech at Strom Thurmond's 100th birthday party in December 2002. "I want to say this about my state: When Strom Thurmond ran for president, we voted for him. We're proud of it. And if the rest of the country had followed our lead, we wouldn't have had all these problems over all these years." "All these problems" was Senator Lott's code phrase for the factor that race now plays in American politics, especially in Mississippi. Forty years ago, few would have openly despaired about the senator's declaration, since racially coded speech was common and acceptable. Even when Senator Lott made a similar declaration in 1980, no one said a word. Now that the veil has been lifted off the era of Mississippi's Sovereignty Commission, everyone, not just a chosen few, can decipher the code.

It's uncomfortable, to say the least, to witness the mentality of the segregationist era at work. What reassures me is that the powers of justice and redemption are harder at work among the people in Mississippi than these forces of the past. I know it, I feel it, I see it.

Months passed after my trip to Mississippi with Patrick and Aidan before I returned there. It didn't take long before I felt compelled to travel back to what my kids thought was a very cool place. Almost three years to the day after my first trip back in November 1999, with the exuberance of a child at Christmastime I boarded a plane to Jackson. This time, I made no promises to keep my distance from Mississippi. I needed to be close to it again. I wanted to breathe Southern air and stand on Mississippi ground. Washington felt cool and crisp in the fall. The same season in Mississippi, I knew, would hold a distinctive damp warmth hanging in the air. I couldn't wait to feel it.

As the plane descended into Jackson, I looked out the window and saw a broad expanse of hills and pine trees that speak "Mississippi" like no other place. Jackson spreads across the middle of that belt almost like a blanket, with a few urban landmarks amidst the sprawl in what is still largely a rural state. There is the Gothic white marble Lamar Life tower at its center, jutting out of the middle of downtown, its purple clock face gleaming. When the building was completed in 1925, it was dubbed Jackson's first skyscraper, although it is only thirteen stories high. Without a doubt, it is my favorite building in Jackson. As a child, its imposing height reminded me that I was outside of my usual country environs. Now the tower welcomes me back to Mississippi, with its glowing white marble appearing to signal a greeting.

Though the city lights of Jackson greet me, I am still a country boy at heart. My path back to Mississippi on this trip and every other one takes me back to my hometown of Mount Olive and Covington County. In spite of all the things that have changed there, it is still the place I feel at home, for there is much in its landscape that remains frozen in a time capsule. As I drive back along winding country roads, I stop and talk to old friends, oftentimes swapping stories with them of where I've been the last few years. As the storytelling ends, inevitably I am asked when I'll be back. I assure them that it will be soon. Unlike the many times I have said that before, I mean it now.

This time as I drive around Covington County, it dawns on me that Mississippi is a place that comes alive in its stories. And there are so many great stories here. In every corner of this state, these stories live on. Some remain the same from generation to generation; others change. Whether folks in Mississippi like it or not, the Sovereignty Commission is one of their stories, part of their cultural lore. Within its files there are tons of stories; most of them are tales some Mississippians do not want told about their state, for they are filled with hate and deceit. But they must not be kept buried or forgotten because they speak of a dark past. The stories in the files often tell us as much about the present as they do about the past. At their core, each of them have common elements with every other Mississippi story: parts that can move you to tears in their poignancy, while at the same time making you clench your fists in anger. Once your anger quells, you find something in these tales that makes you laugh in spite of yourself.

As the stories move from the sins of the past to the seeds of redemption in the present, the rhythm of the tales moves you to get up and dance for joy. As the dancing begins, one story ends and another begins.

The story of Mississippi is one that never ends. It echoes through every bend of its winding rivers and across every inch of land within its borders. I'm glad I came back to hear these stories. For better or for worse, they are now a part of my lore. Most of all, I want to keep them alive because the lessons they hold must never be forgotten. And there's much about Mississippi that I'm still learning from them. I'll be back to listen to them again and again, because I know that the really good part is coming right up.

Acknowledgments

Writing a book like this one is never a solitary exercise. On this three-year journey, a number of people supported me along the way and made my work run smoothly. Martha Kaplan, my agent and friend, guided me as I developed the concept for the book and believed in it, even at times when I did not. My editor, Elizabeth Carduff, kept me on the right track as I wrote and helped me ask myself the hard questions about life in Mississippi. Evie Righter copyedited the manuscript with great skill and care. I owe a sincere debt of gratitude to all of them.

The voyage back to Mississippi would not have been possible without the love, support, and encouragement of my wife Colleen Delaney Eubanks. From pushing me to write down my thoughts on the very day I discovered my parents' names in the Sovereignty Commission files to listening to the same stories time and again as I teased them apart (as well as enduring my numerous trips south), she was with me every step of the way. The inquisitiveness and wisdom of our children, Patrick, Aidan, and Delaney, forced me to dig deeper into a subject that for years I only explored on the surface. Thank you for helping me bridge the infinite distance.

My mother, Lucille Richardson Eubanks, always stood a phone call away and served as a font of information as I explored old ties. Thank you for not revealing too much and making me answer my questions for myself. My sisters, Sharon, Gretta, and Sylvia, helped me sift through old family photographs and loaned me their favorite pictures. As I walked the ground of our old farm, I often felt their childhood presences beside me.

As the book took shape, my good friend Frederick Reuss served as a sounding board for ideas along the way and reviewed the first chapters of the book, for which I am most grateful. Later, as the book grew, E. Ethelbert Miller gave me writing tips as well as his poet's touch.

On each trip to Mississippi, veteran journalist Bill Minor helped me place my book in the context of the fifty years he covered Mississippi politics. I am grateful for the time and energy he devoted to each of our discussions, for I learned much from them. Jerry Mitchell of the Jackson *Clarion-Ledger* willingly shared his invaluable insights into the world of the Sovereignty Commission and became both a source of information and a friend. In addition to arranging Patrick and Aidan's "grand tour" of Ole Miss, Ron Bartlett generously gave me books from his Mississippi history collection, including the copy of *Mississippi: The Closed Society* he bought before his journey to Mississippi from Utah.

Archivists became my friends as I looked for connections to the net of information I found in the Sovereignty Commission files. I am especially grateful to the staff of the reading room of the Mississippi Department of Archives and History, especially Clarence W. Hunter. I also extend a special note of thanks to Toby Graham and the staff of the McCain Library at the University of Southern Mississippi for guiding me through the Paul B. Johnson Family Papers. Thanks to Jennifer Ford and the staff of the Special Collections Room of the Williams Library at the University of Mississippi, who helped me through the papers of James Meredith and Russell Barrett.

Ed King, Horace Harned, and Denson Lott made the world I experienced in the archives come to life. Thank you all for being open and honest.

Vincent Virga gave me much-needed assistance in picture editing and made me dig around for just the right images for the photo section. Danny Lyon suggested photographs from his days in Mississippi as a photographer for SNCC. When I found few visual materials on my hometown in archives, old friends in Mount Olive came to the rescue, particularly Jim and Kathy Brewer and Word Johnston. Thank you for turning Mount Olive upside down in your search of the right photos for me.

Special thanks to Reverend Francis Cosgrove and Reverend Brian Kaskie, who always gave me a home away from home in Jackson, as well as a quiet place to write and think. June and Jackie Barron generously provided me a home in Mount Olive again and, along with Madison and Mary Helen Magee, helped me remember much that I had forgotten about the place and the people of Covington County.

As I wandered around Mississippi and kept Mississippi in my mind after returning to Washington, lots of people talked with me along the way. All of them kept me from getting lost, whether I was on the road or at my computer. I am especially grateful to Ben Castle, Donald Cole, John Dittmer, Bill Ferris, Luberta Adams Johnson, Alice and Julius Magee, Helen Ruth McInnis, Jesse and Geraldine Parker, Homer Powell, Andrew Reeves, Scott and Miriam Rone, David Sansing, Tammy Smith, and Alvin Williams. Thank you all.

And finally, I want to thank my father, Warren Eubanks, for making me his country-road traveling companion. A backseat view can provide a window to the world.